EFFECTIVE

STORYTELLING

STEP BY STEP

Captivate, Engage, and Influence your Audience

O. G. GOAZ

Every effort has been made to trace copyright holders and to obtain their permission for the use of copyright material. The publisher apologizes for any errors or omissions in the above list and would be grateful if notified of any corrections that should be incorporated in future reprints or editions of this book.

osnatgoaz@poprite.co.il

Translated from Hebrew by Nina Luskin
Editing by Robin Marcus and Dr. Mary S. Lederer
Cover by Studio Lilach Gonen

* * *

CONTENTS

All the clips featured in the book can be viewed at
https://www.poprite.co.il/storytellingebook

Please note that each clip is preceded by a brief explanatory text. For maximum benefit, we strongly suggest that the reader take a few moments to read it before viewing the clip.

All the links were tested prior to publication. If nonetheless you find a link that is faulty or no longer valid, kindly notify us and we will address the problem.

1

Prologue

Our lives are filled with stories – stories that define us, stories that define our existence. Stories that, time and again, as a matter of course, we tell to ourselves and to people who surround us: at home, in the street, in a social setting, at work. We have all experienced disappointments; we have all experienced success; we all have aspirations, dreams, apprehensions, fears.... All these raw materials are at our disposal, the stuff that good stories are made of.

Whether you are a leader seeking to promote an idea, a public speaker hoping to leave a mark on the hearts and minds of your listeners, a business owner or content marketer endeavoring to present the advantages of a product or service – remember: If you wish to engage and influence your audience, you must enliven your discourse with stories. And not just any stories, but those that have the power to boost your agenda and to advance the goals and objectives that you have set.

I could tell you about my childhood on the outskirts of Haifa, Israel; about my grandparents' home, where I grew up; about my coming into maturity at a restricted military base in the south of Israel, in the middle of nowhere; about my travels to every corner of the world that began on a ship bound for the Far East; about my professional training at a Tel Aviv advertising agency; about my work as a spokeswoman and communications adviser, and my encounters with various public and political figures; about my doctoral thesis, unfinished but not forsaken; and even about my everyday life in Israel's capital, Jerusalem.

Yet although, just like you, I have thousands upon thousands of stories to tell, enough to fill reams of paper, the only stories that you will find in the pages of this book are the ones that demonstrate the use of stories as a strategic tool to promote one's agenda, goals, and objectives, in life, at work, and in business.

2

A True Story

On November 5, 2006, while driving south on a one-way road in the family car, we were hit from the left by a vehicle that had crossed the intersection on a red light. Our car turned around on its axis several times, shot towards a traffic island, and came to a standstill.

I remember these moments well, the moments of the crash. I remember feeling as if time had stopped. I remember my first desperate scream – "Avi, no! No! No!" – as if words alone could avert the inevitable. I remember thrusting my arm forward inside the car, as if I had the power to buffer the impact of the crash. I remember lurching out of the car and collapsing on the traffic island; seeing strange people running in my direction – my brain registering their movements in slow motion as one of them extricated my daughters from their car seats and brought them to me – and that took an eternity. I remember looking them over, from head to toe – this time, in fast motion – and feeling calmer. The younger, age two, had a nosebleed. The older, age five, had smashed her forehead.

I remember looking inside the car and seeing my husband

Avi, his head flat on the steering wheel and blood running down the side of his face, to his jaw. I remember thinking that he was dead. I remember that two paramedics rushed towards me; I saw their mouths move and understood that they were asking me something, but I couldn't understand what. I remember that I had difficulty breathing, that I was placed on a stretcher and had an oxygen mask put over my face, that a policeman approached us and after taking one look at me addressed my older daughter, that she said something in reply, her face contorted with confusion, or was it dread?

I remember how, afterwards, she told me that he had said her father had asked what her and her sister's names were.

I remember the feeling of helplessness as I was lifted into the ambulance, my two daughters seated next to me, crying; how I looked them in the eyes in an attempt to calm them down. I remember that, after more than two hours of tests and X-rays, I finally saw Avi, lying on a bed, fully conscious. That when he recognized me, he launched into a barrage of questions that seemed to me strange and incoherent. I remember that, nevertheless, I answered every one of them in turn. But he asked the same questions again. And again. And again. As if I had not given him any replies at all. I remember that I couldn't understand what was wrong with him and burst out in uncontrollable sobs. I remember how, on coming home – just me and my daughters – I resolved to go on as usual, no matter what. But I also remember how extremely difficult this turned out to be.

* * *

In a month or so, I went back to work for the first time and handed in my resignation letter. I felt that the family trauma we had all gone through compelled me to do that. That I must be disengaged. Free to take care of myself, to take care of my daughters, to take care of my family. That I could not continue living as if nothing had happed, continue chasing god knows what, day after day. Resume the marathon of life, the hectic routine. Become once more an irritable and busy mother. Take up the same petulant refrain that holding an intensive, full-time job and being a mother is like working two-and-a-half jobs and earning less than three-quarters of one salary. Carry on my back – at every given moment – a thousand-ton load of guilt.

At that time, I worked as a spokeswoman for the national public authority, and on my head, where an ear was supposed to be, was a cellphone. Attached to my belt was a gnarled beeper. I was one of those career women who believe that if they are not available day and night, holidays and weekends, seven days a week, twenty-four hours a day, anywhere, under any circumstances, the world – or at the very least their job – would go to pieces.

And then, as if with the flash of a sword – everything stopped.

After nearly twenty years of zealously chasing the clock, in a matter of hours I turned into one of those women who seemingly do little other than hang out the wash. Scrub the surfaces in the kitchen and stack the dishwasher. Cook and clean. I became a mother and a housewife – a full-time one, too. And so the years passed. Another and another. And another.

And then one day, I woke up and realized that I had become my own shadow, someone whose life does not really belong to her. That I had turned into a type of person I had never wanted to become. And I was ashamed of what had become of the woman who had always prided herself on her panache.

I – who in the army had been an acclaimed sports and krav maga (self-defense) instructor; who held an MA in communication and journalism, in both applied and research tracks; whose name had been posted on the Dean's List; a student teacher at the Hebrew University; an intern at one of

Israel's leading advertising agencies; a marketing consultant; a public relations manager; a popular blogger; a communications adviser; a public authority spokeswoman; someone who had raced around the Israeli Parliament building to mastermind a neighborhood protest – I had metamorphosed into a full-time housewife.

I felt so ashamed that soon afterwards I started a doctorate, just so that if people on the street or in a supermarket should ask me what I did, I wouldn't have to say "nothing."

For almost seven years I was, in my view, a housemaid.

And during that seventh year of "nothing," as if I hadn't yet had enough, my mother passed away. She died of breast cancer at the age of sixty-four, ten years after her own mother had succumbed to the same illness. I sank into a kind of melancholy. I began pondering statistics, thinking of getting my affairs in order, and wondering what my own chances might be in this game…. In other words, when would it be my turn?

And then, one morning, I told Avi that if I didn't do something with my life, I would also become ill. I was feeling pain in my joints and bones, and I truly believed that I was in an advanced stage of terminal illness.

That day, as usual, I went to the local library to exchange books for my eldest daughter. Even though our membership covered only children's books, a book for adult readers displayed at the entrance to the library caught my attention. It was a volume by Timothy Ferris, entitled *The 4-Hour Workweek*. Although I had never heard of the book or its author, and although at that time I didn't read anything unrelated to my PhD studies, I felt a strange compulsion to borrow that book. I picked it up and placed it between two of the fantasy paperbacks I had picked out for my daughter, hoping the librarian wouldn't notice that it wasn't a children's book. The librarian scanned all the books, stamped them, and reminded me to return them within thirty days. I breathed a sigh of relief.

Soon after, for the first time in many years, I was engrossed in a volume that was not a reference book, a textbook, or a manual. I devoured the book in several hours, spread over three days – after all, I was still a housewife and full-time mother. That book – or more precisely, the sequence of events in the aftermath of my reading it – changed my life.

How is that possible? It's as simple as this: I thought to myself that maybe I could combine work and taking care of my children and my home. Maybe I could be the kind of mother who is always there for her children, while at the same time doing something with my life, something for myself. Maybe I was able to avoid being only a mother or only a career woman. Maybe it was possible to find a path between those two extremes, to find my own way. Maybe I could be both, and still keep my sanity.

Yet this epiphany was immediately followed by the realization that there was a serious problem. Even with all my experience and know-how, all my flair, for seven whole years I had been outside the world of working life.

So how could I start using my abilities and skills after having been so completely outside of the game? After years of sitting on the bench – and at the age of forty-five, to boot – who would consider returning me to the playing field?

Especially since, during those seven years, the world had changed so fundamentally. With the advent of new technology, the entire sphere of marketing, advertising, and public relations that had been so familiar to me had been radically transformed. The place of traditional media – the press, the television, the radio – had been taken over by the internet, most notably social media. And how well was I prepared for this new era? I didn't even have a Facebook profile! And certainly no account on Twitter or Instagram.

So what the hell was I to do?

And then, almost in despair, I thought, why not check out

what it's all about? Just scratch the surface? Maybe it's not as bad as it seems.

After putting my girls to bed one evening, I ensconced myself in front of the computer, plugged in my earphones, and started searching Facebook for clips on digital marketing. The first clip that came up was entitled "The Ultimate Guide to Facebook Advertising."

I clicked on the link and started to watch. The clip featured a woman considered a guru on everything to do with Facebook, and in the video she related how, from being a housewife – and a full-time mother of triplets – she had become an expert on Facebook and the main breadwinner in the family. What struck me most was what she said at minute 4:42 of the clip: "I found a book called *The 4-Hour Workweek*. I read it ... in like three days."

That book had changed her life.

"The Ultimate Guide to Facebook Advertising" (Link 1)

This was the first clip I had come across, out of the millions on YouTube. Of the infinite amount of content on the net, on my first search, I had gravitated to a clip whose narrator relays how, following her husband's breakdown, she had been transformed from a housewife into an expert on Facebook marketing – by reading the very same book I had picked up on instinct at the library.

Justifiably or not, I saw this as a portent – a sign from heaven – in spite of being a secular person not in the least given to mysticism. Something about this coincidence had caused me to raise an eyebrow and wonder: was it really a coincidence?

Regardless of how logical it may have been, I saw a message in that coincidence. And at that moment, I resolved to pick up the gantlet and do what I knew best: study.

For exactly three months and twenty-one days, every second of my free time was devoted to researching and studying advertising and marketing in the digital age. On some days I didn't go to bed until the small hours of the morning. Occasionally I forgot to or didn't have time to eat and drink. There were nights when I slept for three or four consecutive hours at best – because only after putting my daughters to bed in the evening was I able to catch up on my research, and because often my overwrought mind wouldn't stop thinking. Even my dreams were about that stuff, and every free minute of my time was spent surfing the internet.

I read every study, every post, every book on the subject that I could get a hold of. I consumed every bit of content that touched upon the world of advertising and marketing in general, and modern digital technology in particular. I pored over research into social and human behavior, particularly economic behavior. I participated in hands-on webinars on internet advertising and watched innumerable YouTube clips about how to manage campaigns on social media. I read tons of texts about advertising and marketing in digital media: in Hebrew, in English, and even – grinding my teeth – a few in French.

If you had given me a text in Circassian and said that it was crucial for understanding the age of modern technology, I would have found a way to get through it. I consumed everything within reach of my hand or mouse. Studies and books, from all over the world, on subjects related to persuading and motivating people; research on rationality, including works by Nobel laureates such as Daniel Kahneman and Amos Tversky.

And then, after more than three months of in-depth study,

a simple idea occurred to me. It was a little past midnight, and the house was very still. I had been watching a clip on YouTube, the last of many that day, but stopped it after about forty-five seconds. I took the earphones out of my ears and grasped my head with both hands. At that moment I understood the only lesson that I needed to learn. As Ecclesiastes had said: "There is nothing new under the sun." What has been will be again.

To be sure, the platforms had changed, but the essence? Human behavior had not changed one iota! I realized that persuading people had always been and still was contingent on analyzing the forces make humans act in one way and not another. That everything I had learned over more than fifteen years of working in marketing communication was still very much valid. And most importantly, I understood that the key to success in the age of modern technology was exactly the same as it had been for eons – understanding human behavior. The rest is nothing but pyrotechnics, cosmetics, and crinkling cellophane wrapping.

I understood that the methods of persuasion and getting a message across, which are at the core of modern marketing strategies, had not really changed, and neither had human or social psychology. That human beings were still human beings.

Say you have an award-winning recipe for carrot cake, but instead of making it in your trusty rectangular Pyrex dish, you now have to use a round metal pan and bake it in a new oven. True, you need to learn how to operate the buttons and account for the idiosyncrasies of the new appliance, to adjust the temperature and baking time and reckon with a few other technicalities, but that's it!

That same night I opened an account on Facebook, and right afterwards on LinkedIn, Google+, Pinterest... and god knows what else. The following morning, I went to the Tax Authority and opened files with the Income Tax, VAT, and Social Security offices. I hired the services of an accountant, and from then on, I have been operating as a strategic storytelling adviser to senior officers, managers, and business owners. And – oh, yes! – I have also written the book that you are reading right now.

And now I would like you to answer a question, frankly, hand on heart: Do you believe that the story I have just recounted really happened?

O. G. GOAZ

3

Telling Stories

Well, I've got news for you. The answer is no. The story I have just told you never happened in reality, for a simple reason: stories, in general, do not occur in reality.

Where, then, do they occur? In our minds!

Stories are, in effect, the product of our interpretation and construction of reality – in line with our understanding of it. That is, in a story that we create, we impose our interpretation on events, and thus actually produce another reality.

Think for a moment. The facts and events at the core of any story that we tell to or about ourselves make up only ten percent of it.

And the remaining ninety percent?

That's our interpretation and understanding of the episode, and not what has actually occurred. The stories we tell ourselves and those around us are therefore, in effect, a reality we have constructed and created. A sort of virtual reality, if you wish.

If the facts, the events, the ten percent – what we will call here the factual grid, the skeleton of our story – have actually happened, and the remaining ninety percent, the stuff that links or wraps them together – what Peter Brooks in his 2002 work *Policing Stories* calls "the narrative glue" – are our own creation, then the final product, the story itself, is more akin to fantasy than to reality.

The narrative glue – that is, the stuff that attaches a fact or an incident to other facts or incidents, or the plot that envelops the event grid – is also what invests the story with internal logic, meaning, and import. Without it, there cannot be a story at all, only a sequence of events and facts. We will discuss this at greater length later on.

What's more, the impact of either of these story elements is not directly proportional to their respective size. That is, the narrative glue, which accounts for the lion's share of a story to begin with, has an even bigger impact on the final product than is implied by the proportion it takes up, at least in terms of its power to influence the addressee.

Why?

Because, in most cases, it is the wrapping that ultimately imbues a story with meaning. The wrapping is what wields the power to convey messages, further agendas, touch the hearts of the audience and keep them in thrall, to promote various aims and objectives, to influence individuals and propel them to action, to shape reality, and even to build an entire universe of values. In other words, the wrapping in which we encase the events, data, and facts is the element that transforms a sequence of incidental occurrences into a story that deserves to be told.

If the narrative glue is missing, there is no story as such – only an agglomeration of data and a sequence of dry facts.

It follows, then, that one could tell dozens of different stories based on the same factual grid, and all of them would be equally true. That is, one can make different covers for the same set of facts and produce a range of true stories even though none of them has occurred in reality.

The story I told you about myself is true, even though it

has never taken place in the real world. This story is a faithful representation of events or incidents in which I have been involved but, like all stories, it occurred only in my mind. Put differently, this story is a reconstruction of events, in line with my agenda and incorporating my subjective interpretation – whether I was aware of my interpretation or not. Through this story I not only understood what actually happened but also constructed it, thereby effectively creating it anew. It is obvious, then, that I could have used its factual grid, the dry data, to tell an altogether different true story. And not just one, but scores.

Let's try it. Let's take the story that I told you, pull it apart, and isolate its core facts:

1. Name: Osnat Goaz.
2. Status: Married with children.
3. Army service: Sports trainer and krav maga instructor.
4. Education: MA in communication and journalism.
5. Specialization: Public relations and advertising.
6. Experience: Student teacher at the Hebrew University, public relations manager, spokeswoman for the public authority, communications adviser, marketing consultant.
7. Events: Involved in a car accident, mother passed away as a result of cancer.
8. Currently: Freelancer in marketing and consulting.

Using the above facts as a skeleton, I could tell you the following story:

> Hi, my name is Osnat Goaz, and I am a trained marketing consultant with an MA in communication and journalism from the Hebrew University; I am married with three children, all girls.
>
> I started my own business, a marketing consulting company, after having accrued thirteen years of hands-on experience in the field of

marketing communication, specializing in public relations and advertising. My resolution to open a company of my own, rather than go back to work for someone else, as I had done throughout my adult life, stemmed from a number of reasons. The main event that precipitated this decision was a car accident approximately ten years ago in which I was involved and which made me realize very clearly that life was too short and too irreversible to go back to work as an employee. This, and possibly also my mother's sudden death from cancer at a relatively young age, is what helped me understand that, in one's life, one should try to achieve some kind of personal satisfaction. As a result, after a break of several years, I decided to return to the labor market, albeit on my own terms.

I explored the secrets of digital advertising and discovered that storytelling has the power to drive winning marketing strategies for companies, businesses, and organizations. Then I opened my own business and wrote a book about the use of story as a strategic tool.

So what do you think?

Even a cursory comparison of the two stories shows that the facts that constitute them are identical. What is different? The "getup," the wrapping, the narrative glue. Something that links facts to other facts. And voilà: two different stories.

Are both of them true?

Definitely, even though neither has actually occurred in reality.

How come?

Because stories, in general, do not occur in reality; only the facts at their core do.

You are probably saying to yourself, wait a minute, in the second story she added facts that are not mentioned in the first, and omitted others that are.

And that is true: A story also contains what is omitted from it – what we choose to leave out.

Let me illustrate what I mean. Take a look at the picture below:

Photo courtesy of veronicascornucopia.com

The missing slice defines the cake, no less than the cake itself – and if you think about it, maybe even more so. Why is that?

Because in addition to defining the cake, the missing piece also tells us a story about it: Someone has cut the cake and maybe has eaten a piece.

It is important to understand that when we tell a story, we do not recount everything that has happened to us, second by second: rather, at every juncture we decide which facts to include; we select what is important and what is trivial to the story; we weigh what is more revealing when left out, what will advance our storyline and what will hamper it, what will enhance the message that we wish to get across and what will sabotage it. We consider what will advance our agenda and our purpose and what might have the opposite effect, what will render the story more "tellable" and what will make it boring and fit to be shelved forever.

This rationale is based on the Aristotelian teleological principle in which the various stages of a creative process will always be subordinate to the purpose, which the former is designed to achieve. According to this approach, the choice of how to present events is governed by a pre-determined climactic point, and events are then presented in a causal sequence that leads to this apex. According to this principle, a biased or partial presentation of facts does not by any means constitute a flaw. In fact, if you were to attempt to faithfully represent in detail everything that had occurred, you'd end up with an inferior narrative texture that would appear trivial, trite, and unfit to be told.

I place so much emphasis here because it is important to make clear that each of us possesses a vast arsenal of stories, that each event we experience has the potential to open up a whole world of stories.

In other words, every incident that we have experienced is loaded with a boundless variety of possibilities, and focusing on one aspect while disregarding others will give rise to a story that cements a particular worldview. And if every story that we tell includes both facts that are relayed and those that are omitted, it is possible to tell a number of substantively different stories based on the same factual framework. Invariably, our choice of what to tell and what to omit will be biased, whether or not we are aware of this.

One statement that I hear over and over again from clients, colleagues and other people interested in storytelling is "I have nothing to tell!" And that is nothing but balderdash, stuff, and nonsense! It's not that you have nothing to tell; you simply don't know why, what, or how.

But don't worry, I will deal with that in due course.

4

The Stories That We Choose To Tell

However, before I elaborate on the details and implications of the above questions – what exactly to tell, how to tell, and why tell at all – I would like to briefly direct the spotlight to which stories we choose to tell in any given case. It is a crucial element in understanding the power of a story, so let's retrace our steps.

I have told you two personal stories about myself, based on a selection of facts taken from real life. But even if I had included all the facts from the first story in the second one, without adding or subtracting anything, I would still have been able to tell you an altogether different story, convey entirely different messages, forge different meanings, and divert the focus to different places.

Why is all this so important? Why do I have to repeat it and drum it in?

Simply because there is great significance in which story we choose to tell.

The act of telling stories is central to our lives. Telling

stories is the most fundamental and ancient means at our disposal as human beings to understand reality, to make sense of events, to shape our memories, to build our identities, whether personal or collective, to convey sensations, to establish coherence... and to construct reality. The stories we tell serve to transmit knowledge, define identity, account for phenomena, interpret events, make sense of situations, set up causal relations, and justify our behaviors.

Put differently, stories are tools that impart meaning to everything that happens to us in life, every occurrence. But remember: it is the stories that impart meaning, not the reality as such!

Crucially, these stories we tell ultimately define us, relegate us to categories, and stamp us with a label. That is because we tell them not only to ourselves but also to those around us – at business meetings, social gatherings, lectures, presentations; over coffee and cake in a local coffee house; to friends, colleagues, passers-by; briefly, to a woman next door who is just parking her car; to our nuclear and extended families; to those dear to us who are far away and to strangers who are nearby; to friends and enemies; to anyone with whom we have any kind of interaction. In any circumstances, through any channel, in any mode – face-to-face, over the phone, by mail, via social media, on Skype, through chats...

Even though stories have such enormous power, how come we tell them relentlessly, using every possible medium, and without a moment's respite? We don't even stop to think what it is we are telling; we don't reflect on why or how we are doing this. So why do we not tell our stories consciously, with awareness, with a predefined intention?

This is a critical point.

We can and must choose what to tell – what to recount to ourselves and what to reveal to those around us. And we may tell stories that are entirely different from the ones we thought we were telling in the first place, possibly without giving it much thought.

If stories have such a great impact on our lives, shouldn't we choose which stories to tell and thereby get a measure of control over the ways in which they define us? What stories should we tell so as to influence how others see us? And what stories could we tell to influence the way others see reality – for example, our children?

But wouldn't making such a decision mean that we are lying to ourselves? Lying to others?

No, it wouldn't. Because if the only true element in all stories that we tell is their factual framework, while everything else is our interpretation, our construction of reality, then the story is essentially a product of our overwrought imagination! As psychologist Jerome Bruner aptly noted in his 1991 journal article "The Narrative Construction of Reality," stories are a means through which human cognition comprehends and interprets reality, and they cannot be either refuted or validated. To render this philosophical discussion less abstract, I will give you an example from real life.

Several years ago, as I mentioned earlier, I embarked on a doctorate. My dissertation, at least in the beginning, dealt with stories in business periodicals.

My supervisor was an eminent professor of international renown, important and respected in academia.

After nearly one-and-a-half years of hard but frustrating work writing a research proposal, the long-awaited day arrived when the members of my dissertation committee – all of them likewise senior academics and leading researchers in their respective fields – gave me the green light. Finally, I had reached the stage at which my proposal, approved and signed by the dissertation committee, would go to the research institute to be stamped, thus rendering the committee's de facto endorsement officially valid. It should be noted that this stage is considered a procedural formality;

as one academic old-timer told me, "You can now stop worrying: this is merely a symbolic ritual."

As you can imagine, I was in seventh heaven.

At long last, my proposal had been approved, and now – full steam ahead! I was very happy also (if not mainly) because I hadn't had an easy time getting to that point. Actually, it was quite hard. Very, very hard. I know: Many PhD students will tell you that doing a doctorate is not easy. But in my case it was exceptionally difficult.

Not because I was no longer in my twenties – and in fact at least twice that age.

And not because I had a family – a husband and three children, one of them a very young baby.

And not because, as I navigated between my home, my children, the babysitter, diapers, the kids' extracurricular activities, driving to and fro, handling studies, viruses, assignments, and tutorials, I sometimes felt as if my life were a series of somersaults, backward and forward.

And not because going back to academic studies after a break of over fifteen years, sharing a lecture-hall bench with kids fresh from army service, made me feel completely out of touch.

And not because finding a supervisor under such circumstances, when your life is completely outside of the academic environment, is nearly impossible.

And not even because my mother had just been diagnosed with breast cancer, exactly ten years after her mother – who for all intents and purposes had been my mother too, having raised me from the time I was a baby – had died from the same illness.

But because, before the committee finally approved my research proposal, I had written a number of proposals that had been rejected over and over again.

Because during that entire period, I had lived in a continuous state of puzzlement: Where do I go wrong, time and time again? What is it that I fail to understand? And mainly – why?

Because at the end of that journey, I reached the inevitable conclusion that I must be made of the wrong stuff, or maybe I had lost the strength I had always prized. Strength that had helped me overcome, all on my own, a serious and undiagnosed problem with writing; had won me the title of "Outstanding Soldier" in my krav maga course, out of fifty male and five female participants; had seen me sent to train combat soldiers before they went to the battlefield; had helped me finish my degree with honors; had won me the role of student teacher at the Hebrew University; had put my name on the Dean's List.

Or maybe I had never had it to begin with?!

This self-judgment had brought me to my knees. My self-perception as someone who in everything related to studies had almost always had it relatively easy was shattered against an obstacle at the most basic stage of my degree, which I had not been able to overcome.

So when that day finally arrived – the day the documents were sent to the research institute to be stamped as a matter of form, rendering my research proposal officially approved – I was on cloud nine. There was no one in the whole world happier than I.

And then, about two weeks later, came the eagerly awaited letter from the research institute. I remember that morning well: how I opened the envelope with trembling fingers. Not because I feared what it contained, for I knew there was nothing to worry about, but because at long last the moment had come for which I had worked so hard. I unfolded the letter, which laconically informed me, in black and white, that regrettably, the research institute had been compelled to reject my PhD research proposal.

How was that possible? Was it conceivable that five members of the dissertation committee – leading professors among them – had approved a proposal, and the research institute was rejecting it? By what right?

I immediately got in touch with one of the university's lecturers whom I knew well. He was even more shocked than I and said that, in more than twenty years in academia, he had never heard of a case in which a research institute failed to endorse a PhD proposal that had been approved by the dissertation committee.

For me, that letter was a resounding slap in the face. I felt the insult scorching my insides. I saw a story of failure sprouting within me, this time stamped with an impervious red wax seal.

During those weeks my mother's condition declined as well, and even though I was still in the denial stage, deep inside I knew that this was it, this was the end. Again I had to prepare to part from a mother, the second time around, and because of the same accursed illness.

Shaken to the core and with a bitter taste in my mouth, I set myself to work again, albeit without any confidence in my abilities, and tried to fix what I believed was irreparable, to reach what I believed was inaccessible. I told myself that everything was lost, and no PhD would come out of me. My relationship with my supervisor deteriorated even further, becoming crippled beyond hope.

Shortly after, following an upsetting telephone conversation with my supervisor on the way back from dropping my youngest daughter at her nursery school, I finally caved in. In a fluster, I wrote my supervisor an email announcing that I wouldn't continue to pursue the degree.

Although I was convinced that I had made the right decision, somewhere deep in my heart I hoped that my supervisor would ask me to reconsider, would say that she was not prepared to give up on me. That in the state I was in at the time, I ought not to make such a decision. That I must give it a second thought. But my email sank into oblivion like a stone in a silent sea. I received no response, positive or negative.

Several months later, at another branch of the university,

where I went to meet a friend for a coffee, I saw my supervisor standing at the entrance to one of the buildings. She looked at me with what I thought was resentment, and I couldn't understand why. I looked directly into her eyes. And then I realized that her look was not rancorous but simply vacant – opaque and inscrutable. A look that did not betray any recognition, as if I were a stranger. She was looking through me: to her I was transparent.

I continued toward the coffee house, my eyes fixed on hers. Possibly, deep down, in spite of everything, I had expected some sort of reaction, maybe a slight nod, a flicker of recognition. Yet I couldn't detect any response.

It wasn't a good time for me. I spent those days walking around with a great void inside, a feeling that, even today, years later, hits me in the core when the subject of my doctorate comes up.

And then, one evening, several months after that encounter, I came across a Facebook feed saying that my supervisor had passed away after a long illness.

Alzheimer's.

All of a sudden, the picture came into focus, and my story took a sharp turn. At that point, I understood a lot of things about myself. About her. About my relationship with her. At last, all the puzzle pieces fell into place, and everything became clear, like sunlight on a bright, hot summer afternoon. In place of anger and humiliation came sorrow and forgiveness. Heartache for her. Heartache for myself. Grief over what might have been and never was, and will never come to pass.

I realized that all that time – more than a year of shuttling back and forth, of miscommunication, of the incessant ping-pong of text messages, telephone conversations, meetings, of the breakdown in the relationship, of waiting in vain for responses, of frustration, of feeling totally unable to understand anything – I had been telling a harsh story about myself. And I realized that I could have been telling myself an altogether different story. I am not saying that the other story, when told, has eased the pain. I am still hurting, but much less so. And above all, it is no longer the kind of pain that consumes everything good inside you, destroys you from within. One that is always whispering in your ear: "You are a failure."

Does this mean that the PhD story I am telling myself today is more true than the previous one?

By no means. It is as true as the one that I was telling myself before, because both stories are based on events that have occurred in reality. They differ only in my interpretation of these facts, the narrative glue, the "fabulaic wrapping" that I used to invest the incidents with meaning in order to link one fact to the next, each to the one that succeeded it.

If you think that all the other scholars involved in my PhD proposal would tell you my story or, for that matter, my supervisor's, think again.

Although facts remain facts, the wrapping through which they are communicated will be completely different for each one of these narrators. Each will create an entirely different story, imparting a unique meaning to facts that are incontestable, to incidents that have occurred in reality.

And what will account for the main difference between the versions?

The framing effect!

5

The Framing Effect

Before discussing this phenomenon in depth, let me illustrate its far-reaching impact on the stories we tell ourselves and others.

I need you to imagine a podium.

A podium at the Olympic Games.

The first place. The second place. The third place. Three champions mount the podium.

Which of them is the happiest?

Quite obviously, the one who has won first prize. He is the world champion. He will receive a gold medal. He is one of a kind. A champion among champions.

And who is the next happiest?

The second, you will surely say.

And that's the thing – it's not him.

Studies have shown that the most gratified person after the first-place winner is the one who has won third place. You heard right – the bronze medalist is usually much happier than the silver medalist.

Maybe this will strike you as paradoxical; maybe you will think it is illogical, but when push comes to shove, common sense and logic have nothing to do with it.

The thing that holds sway here is the framing effect; in other words, what is relevant is the reference point, aka the adaptation point. In this situation, each of the three champions tells himself a different story. The same reality, the same facts, but three different stories.

The one who finished third mounts the podium, looks down and says to himself, "Yay!!!" or something like that. "I have made it to the top, one of the three!" On the other hand, the one who finished second looks up and tells himself, "Oh, shit! I could have been a world champion!"

The story that each of the athletes on the podium tells himself is categorically different. The three stories are based on the same facts, which are incontrovertible and indisputable. What is different is the reference point, with the result that the story each champion tells himself is completely different from the other two.

If you still have doubts regarding the tremendous power of the framing effect, I suggest that you familiarize yourself with the research of two Israeli scholars, Amos Tversky and Daniel Kahneman, cognitive psychologists who won the Nobel Prize for economics. (More precisely, it was Kahneman who received the prize, because by that time Tversky was no longer alive.)

Tversky and Kahneman's research demonstrates that people are susceptible to the framing effect, in the sense that their preferences and choices depend on the way information is presented to them.

To support that claim, they recount a case that has become known as the "Asian Disease Problem," involving experiments they conducted with student participants. Results show that a person can be led to adopt a certain perspective, or reference point, depending on how the facts are presented. The researchers contend that the influence of framing stems from a cognitive illusion resulting from the way a problem is formulated.

Perhaps this led Neil Postman, in his book *Amusing*

Ourselves to Death (1985), to assert that American businessmen discovered, long before the rest of us, that the quality and usefulness of their goods are subordinate to the art of their display. In other words, the way one forms one's attitudes depends on how information is presented. And let me add here that the mantle in which we wrap the information (the facts, the events) is what shapes the meaning of what we are telling; it will determine our own interpretation of what caused the events narrated and even more so the interpretation of those who will hear our story.

This is also the premise behind a theory Peter Brooks advances in his book *Policing Stories* (2002): that narration is what creates a story's meaning, over and above the facts it incorporates. Brooks exemplifies this thesis through a well-known rape incident that was presented, in appellate courts in the United States, in four totally different versions – or, to use the author's own words, as "different retellings of what we know is the 'same' story," all based on the same set of indisputable facts. Accordingly, they gave rise to four different decisions "starkly opposed to one another."

So, tell me: If we are indeed in a position to choose what to tell and what to omit, and if we have the power to craft a framework that will induce an interpretation of the story's import according to our design…

How, exactly, can this be achieved? How can we put the stories that we tell to good use and make them serve our purposes? How can we use stories to motivate audiences and spur them to action, form worldviews, persuade and influence others? In other words: How can we tell stories that will propel us forward, advance our aims, produce the effect that we set out to achieve, and bring about outcomes that we seek?

Before we attempt to answer these questions, there is one thing we need to agree on: that it is worth our while to tell stories, to take all that trouble, and to invest all that effort.

6

Why Bother Telling a Story?

L et us assume that you are already convinced of the validity of my claim that we each have an arsenal enabling us to tell hundreds, if not thousands, of true stories that may have never occurred in reality.

Our task now is to understand why we should bother telling stories at all.

Why, in your opinion, did I take the trouble to tell you stories about myself?

I could have skipped that part, which – I must confess – was by no means easy to write, and come straight to the point. Yet I decided to tell you my stories. And not just any stories but very revealing ones, stories that put me in a pretty vulnerable position vis-à-vis the reader.

Why?

Because a story is remembered much better than any fact or other data.

Could you estimate how much easier it is to remember a story than to remember facts?

Studies have shown that a story is retained in memory twenty-two times better than any fact.

Here's an example. We have a family game that we usually play on Friday nights and during family car trips. It is a nice memory game, and we all love playing it, especially if there are children present.

It goes like this: Every participant, in turn, says a word, but first they must recite all the words that others have said before, in the right order. The game continues until a long "train" of words accrues. Anyone who makes a mistake, by either omitting a word or mixing up the order, drops out. The winner is the last person who is able to recite all the words in the right order, adding a new word at the end. And even though my memory is much worse than my eldest daughter's, I always win the game.

How do I know that my eldest daughter has a better memory than I?

Maybe because she can cite over 110 decimal digits of π, while I, no matter how hard I try, cannot remember more than five, or at best ten. For heaven's sake, how can one remember dozens of random digits arranged without any logic or order? That's why I am sure that her memory is much better than mine. She can also solve a Rubik's Cube in less than thirteen seconds. And yes, this too is related to memory, in this case, algorithmic memory.

Let us return to our game. In spite of my daughter's impressive mnemonic abilities, I invariably come out the winner in our family word game. The trick is simple: I tell a story. And no matter how bizarre and unrealistic the story, it creates a logical connection, a causal relation – what Nassim Taleb calls in his book *The Black Swan* (2009) "a narrative fallacy." Nevertheless, when my turn comes, all I need to do is reconstruct in my mind the story that I have woven together, saying out loud only the required words according to the order they are nested in the story. Try it yourself! Below I list fifty randomly chosen words, unconnected in any way through logic or context. As you read the words, link them consecutively with the "narrative glue" – that is, tell a story based on them. When you complete the story with the last word on the list, reconstruct all of it in your mind and try to retrieve the words from your memory – according to the sequential order of the story.

Are you ready?

Here are the words:

Morning, cat, airplane, ice cream, garden, chicken, music, computer, path, classroom, lamp, book, earphones, strong, door, kettle, girl, dolphin, hand, apple, soap, black, knife, chocolate, sour, big, opposite, small, plant, blue, beautiful, years, paper, satchel, mobile, microphone, picture, cucumber, banana, saucepan, milk, bird, sea, important, known, alone, sky, good, boat, bathtub.

Now write down the number of words that you were able to recall in the right order.

Below I list another fifty random words. Go over these words once in the order they are listed, with a few seconds' interval between each, and try to remember them by heart. Next, take a sheet of paper, try to retrieve the words from your memory, and write down how many you were able to recall in the right order.

Ready?

Here are the words:

Coffee, bar, platter, vanilla, blooming, yellow, clear, phone, crooked, highway, teacher, library, bad, here, cold, big, lovely, octopus, juice, broom, fork, sweet, bitter, straight, bush, ugly, two, days, tissue, bag, piano, drawing, persimmon, oil, cow, pool, dry, France, foreign, together, orange, pen, key, jar, sugar, bottle, notebook, ticket, umbrella, glass.

So what were the results?

By the way, feel free to add several words of your own choice or make a completely different list.

Next time, play this game with your family or friends – you will see that you can do better than all of them. Just don't divulge the trick and don't forget to tell me what happened.

On a more serious note, when you tell a story, not only does your audience remember better what you have recounted, but you yourself remember much better what you need to say, because a story connects the facts together.

Stories work wonders, do they not?

Because a story can touch you deep to the core.

Let's admit that most of us are not sprightly mathematics professors who get excited, inspired and galvanized at the sight of data and dry facts; accordingly, we can safely assume that it is much more difficult to "touch" and "move" us using freestanding facts or other information of that kind.

Conversely, a story is one of the most powerful tools at the disposal of anyone who wishes to touch people's hearts and minds. This is because a story brings people closer together. A story is in essence a bridge that establishes a connection between people, a bridge that is difficult to build using only facts and data.

Recall for a moment my story, the one I told you at the beginning of the book. You can see for yourself that stories have the power to connect us, total strangers. The stories that I have told you have formed between us a bridge whose foundations are made of empathy and identification, and this bridge has in turn created familiarity and even closeness between you and me, closeness of the kind that couldn't have been achieved through sharing data or relaying an isolated fact.

Sometimes a story moves someone so deeply that it can impel them to support something that contravenes their beliefs. To be sure, it's not easy to do that. It's difficult, even using a story, to make people go along with something that conflicts with their values, but it is within the bounds of possibility.

Here is an incident that I heard about as a child from members of the production team of the play *Anne Frank* and the actors who had taken part in one particular performance.

I remember their story word for word. Even now, I have a mental picture of the actors and the crew seated on the stage and speaking, thoughtfully and soberly. The story they shared with the audience is etched deep in my memory.

They told us how, at the end of one performance during their German tour, an elderly German lady from the audience came up to them and said, "This is horrible, simply horrible! The Nazis shouldn't have killed Anne Frank."

The story of Anne Frank had touched her so deeply that she became convinced that the Nazis had had no business exterminating her.

What about the rest of the Jews? you are probably wondering.

Well, that's a whole different kettle of fish. The lady probably needed to hear their stories before she could decide.

Think about it for a moment.

All fund-raising campaigns – for disaster sites, cancer patients, young diabetics etc. – are anchored in the principle of telling stories that create a sense of identification, empathy, and affinity. We are told a personal story of someone who overcame an illness, regained health and started a family, or of a girl who must prick herself every day dozens of times in order to function on a par with her peers, and we are asked to help her and others like her. These personal stories bring us closer to the protagonist, compel us to identify and empathize with her, and prompt us to help and make a donation. Without such stories, if we are presented with dry facts alone, like "every year, such and such number of people get the illness" and "such and such number of people die from it," it is plausible to assume that most of us would contribute much less. I say "most" because making a donation could depend on several other factors as well, such as a personal acquaintance with someone who is sick, in which case knowing that person's story is in itself enough to impel us to help.

Have you ever watched a TED talk? And if so, have you ever tried to understand the secret of this format, where its power comes from?

Well, I will reveal to you this secret. It is much simpler than you might have thought. The secret of TED speakers' success is their wonderful ability to convey messages through stories. If you scrutinize the clips, you will see that the most successful lectures are those in which the presenter tells a moving story, one that elicits empathy and makes you identify with the speaker, with the subject of the lecture, and with its protagonist. Watch, for example, the following talk from Amy Purdy:

"Living Beyond Limits | Amy Purdy |
TEDxOrangeCoast" (Link 2)

I am sure that you have come across the same effect when viewing reality TV shows.

One of my daughters once told me that whoever wants to win *MasterChef* must think up for themselves a hard and miserable life story, rife with disappointments or failures, or they won't stand a chance of evoking the audience's sympathy.

But contrary to what you might believe, effective stories need not be harsh or sad. There are many other ways to move people by telling stories, and below I will introduce such patterns – what I call the schemas for successful storytelling.

It is of no consequence where you happen to be at the time – with family, friends, or strangers; at a conference facing employees or in a lecture hall in front of a large assembly; in a personal meeting or next to the computer, about to write a post or an article. If you want to touch the hearts and minds of your audience, to persuade and motivate them, you must opt to tell a story anchored in facts. It's a vastly superior method than thesis statements marked by bullets, as in a PowerPoint presentation aggregating dry data devoid of internal coherence.

Because a story helps us to better process complex data.

According to studies carried out in this field, sixty-five percent of participants comprehended and retained facts presented as part of a story, compared with merely five percent who remembered the same facts recounted outside a storyline. The reason is that data and facts are "absorbed" better when woven into a story, that the story renders them part of an associative framework nested in a context.

If we go back to the memory game I described earlier, we will see that one of the reasons we retain facts better when they are part of a story is that associative thinking, or causal contextualization, is humanity's natural mode of thought; by contrast, a sterile recitation of unrelated facts outside of a causal context is, from the brain's perspective, a random activity.

Moreover, a story is an optimal vehicle for conveying difficult or convoluted information, for reducing its complexity, aggregating its constitutive facts, and rendering it more accessible and comprehensible. In other words, a story has the power to make things simpler.

Take, for example, the story of the Apple iPod. Sure, there were other audio devices available before it came on the scene, but they had been advertised using data and facts alone, such as how many giga- or megabytes they could hold. And then came Apple, marketing its iPod with a one-sentence story: "A thousand songs in your pocket."

If you're like me – like most of the general public, with the exception of a small number of computer geeks and gadget lovers – can you really tell what we're supposed to take away from talk about bandwidth and gigabytes?

It's all so abstruse.

Yet, when we are told that a small device that fits into the pocket of our jeans can hold a thousand songs, all we can say is "Wow!"

The above should make it clear that if you want to present an audience with facts, data or complex information, it is preferable to embed them in a storyline.

An education system that adopts a storytelling approach in various disciplines would in all likelihood see much better outcomes. Even in mathematics. Well, I'm not quite sure about calculus – unless a mathematician turns up who can tell a story in numbers.

But consider for a moment young children, at an age when they cannot yet solve an elementary arithmetic exercise. If you formulate a simple math problem as a story – e.g., if you have three balloons and your mom gives you another two balloons, how many balloons will you have altogether? – rather than in the numerical format – i.e., how much is 3 + 2? – the former will always be easier to solve. Try it for yourself.

Because a story creates a frame.

According to sociologist Erving Goffman (1974), framing is an interpretation schema that guides the processing of information. This term is widely used in mass communication research, and the main claim in this regard is that the media frames content in a way that "dictates" a specific, intended meaning or interpretation. In other words, by using verbal and visual means or clues to emphasize certain parts of a story while de-emphasizing or omitting others, and by portraying characters via paradigms that define for the addressee who is "good" and who is "bad," who is "ugly" and so on, the media presents the events in a biased way designed to induce processing along the desired ideological lines.

The use of framing, therefore, makes it possible to direct the addressees' attention to the aspects of a story that we wish to emphasize, and at the same time to downplay, obfuscate, or whitewash those that we would prefer them to disregard.

In other words, a story has the power to promote a preferred agenda or at least to direct and propel processing along a desired channel. It is understandable, then, why many scholars perceive framing as an immensely powerful rhetorical force.

Here's an example of how processing guides an audience towards a preferred interpretation.

Research conducted by Craig McKenzie and Jonathan Nelson (2003) demonstrates that people tend to describe what is presented to them based on how it is framed. In an experiment, two groups of participants were presented with a glass filled halfway with water. One group was told, "Here is a half-full glass of water" and the other, "Here is a half-empty glass of water." Although the glasses contained the same amount of water, participants in each group interpreted the event differently.

Those who were told that the glass was half-empty inferred that the glass had been full to begin with, while those who were told that the glass was half-full inferred that the glass had previously been empty. In other words, the way the glass was described to the participants affected their interpretation of what they had been offered.

That experiment shows that people's understanding of what they are told changes fundamentally depending on the way the information is framed. In this respect, we are talking about the same framing effect as the one demonstrated by Tversky and Kahneman, discussed earlier.

This framing effect in fact underpins an effective psychotherapy technique: by reframing a client's personal story over the course of several sessions, the therapist changes the patient's attitude to life events and thereby also modifies their emotional responses. A similar effect was produced by the revised version of the story I told myself about my unfinished doctorate, as related in the beginning of this book.

Because a story fosters social agreement and coherence.

A story has the power to produce consensus, which is extremely hard to achieve by merely stating facts.

It is much easier to bring about social coherence and agreement using a story, as opposed to reciting dry facts and data, for a story can serve as a kind of "social glue" – it creates a connection, a bridge between complete strangers.

Take, for example, the Old Testament: Have you ever considered that the stories it contains form the foundation of Western culture?

In a similar vein, any society's tradition or history ("his story") is essentially a collection of stories: stories that define its people, connect them with one another, and create an infrastructure for social unity.

Myths, for that matter, also have such a power. Myths are stories that can unite societies, communities and nations. Roland Barthes maintains in his 1972 book *Mythologies* that myths are, in essence, ideological messages that have undergone the process of "naturalization," and as such appear as "a natural condition of the world" even though in fact they are nothing of the kind. Nonetheless, myths join strangers together by fostering coherence and agreement among them.

Because a story draws people's attention.

Would you or anyone else be captivated by a random sequence of facts? How much attention can one expect when presenting dry data?

Conversely, it is relatively easy to capture people's attention with a good story. A good story can and usually does keep people in thrall – this is an indisputable fact. Facts one can hear in any order; it doesn't really matter at which point you start, take a break, or resume. With stories, on the other hand, it is not that simple, because when we listen to a story, we try to follow the events as they unfold and keep track of the plot. There is always a concern that, should our mind wander to other matters and realms, we would find it difficult to catch up, having missed information essential for understanding the whole picture.

And we don't really like feeling adrift, without a clue what others are talking about, do we?

Because a story triggers the release of endorphins.

A story is a format that is familiar to us from early childhood, and some even claim that it is part of our DNA.

This may account for experimental results demonstrating that stories cause chemical changes in our brain.

The researchers who investigated this question suggest that when we listen to a story and form a mental image of its events, our brains release endorphins. Yes, the same substance that is associated with sports, sex, and eating chocolate – the natural drug that alleviates pain, fosters euphoria, and brings about a good mood.

Hopefully, this is a good enough reason for making

storytelling part of any meeting, lecture, or presentation that you may give or lead.

But if you still have doubts on that point, below is a link to a clip that demonstrates the effect of stories on our brain, so you can see for yourself.

"Neuroscience of Business Storytelling" (Link 3)

Because a story creates a mental image.

You probably know the saying "A picture is worth a thousand words." But have you ever considered the worth of a mental image? Not a visual image, but an imaginary one.

A mental image is a picture we create in our minds; it is an imaginary picture – and in my opinion, it is worth at least a thousand visual representations!

So how can we evoke a mental image in the minds of our audience?

By telling them a story. And not just any story but a good one. Our audience will naturally and spontaneously imagine its characters and events. And in a stream of such images, the plot will gradually unfold in their minds.

Everyone who gets entrapped in the web of a story is subject to this unconscious and involuntary process – at least when the story is properly constructed and thus has the power to fire the listeners' imagination. This process occurs every time we read a good book; in effect, we are watching a movie composed of mental images that we create in accordance with our interpretation of the content. And the power of these mental images can be truly tremendous.

Here is an example:

When I gave my middle daughter the second volume of *Anne of Green Gables* (*Anne of Avonlea*), she took one look at it, made a face, and pushed it aside dismissively. I found her reaction puzzling and also felt a little hurt by it.

It is common knowledge – well, at least as far as my daughters are concerned – that the heroines of my childhood, Anne Shirley and Lizzy Bennet, were important in shaping my early perceptions regarding gender equality. So much so that, when my eldest daughter was born, I rushed to buy *Anne of Green Gables* and *Pride and Prejudice*, in spite of my friends' unanimous and rather patronizing admonitions that the chance she would ever read them was slim indeed. And if she did at all, it would be only in ten years or so.

So the reaction of my middle daughter to the book I had given her was somewhat disappointing, and I started to wonder if the excitement she had displayed when I gave her the first volume hadn't been just a show to please me.

When I asked her what was wrong, she replied, "I am not going to read this!"

"But why?" I asked. "Didn't you say that you enjoyed the first part?"

"What do you mean, why?" she retorted, and then, pointing to a brightly colored picture on the cover of the second volume, "Anne Shirley doesn't even look like that!"

My daughter's words made the whole thing crystal clear. There and then I understood how much more powerful an image we create in our minds is than any tangible, material picture.

A few days later, this discovery was confirmed.

It was morning. My eldest daughter was still asleep, and her two sisters were munching something at the breakfast counter in the kitchen. I placed on the stove a small frying pan with a little oil in it. All of a sudden, without any warning, the frying pan caught fire, and the flames shot up all the way to the extractor fan. Following some sort of instinct, I grabbed the frying pan by the handle and threw it into the sink, to the frightened cries of my two daughters.

When their older sister woke up some time later and learned what had happened, for the rest of the day she felt very anxious, and every time I went close to the stove, she became visibly agitated. At some point, I could no longer contain myself and asked her, "Tell me, what's that all about? Your sisters are not as panicky as you, even though they actually saw what happened." And then she said, "That's exactly the point, mom. Don't you know that imagination is stronger than reality?"

The dramatist and screenwriter Jean Anouilh said that "fiction gives life its form." For the purposes of our discussion, we can rephrase that as: It is imagination that gives reality its form.

If you are still in doubt, stop for a moment and try to recall how you felt when you read a book and imagined its protagonist in a certain way, and then a movie came out in which the actor impersonating that character was nothing like the mental image you had created for yourself. How many among you will admit that the movie was disappointing? And your disappointment had nothing to do with how good the movie was or how talented the actors.

I had such an experience after watching *Pride and Prejudice* (2005) starring Keira Knightley and Matthew Macfadyen. Surprisingly, the mental images of Lizzy and Mr. Darcy I'd held in my mind were not those I had summoned while reading the book (probably because that had been twenty-five years earlier); instead, my mind's eye saw Colin Firth and Jennifer Ehle, who starred in the unforgettable 1995 BBC version. In this case, even though the mental image was not mine but a secondhand one, as it were, it was still much too strong for me to accept the new casting of two characters I had long and dearly cherished.

Because storytelling transcends boundaries, whether political, national, or cultural.

Stories are inherently supranational. They cancel out race, gender, and age. They create a bridge between countries and cultures. How so? It is difficult to tell, but a point I made earlier may provide a clue: If someone hears another person's story, they are likely to feel affection and empathy for that person – even if they happen to live in China and speak only Mandarin.

If you are still not convinced, watch these advertisements from Thailand at the link below.

"7 Sad Ads from Thailand – Amazing Thailand Ads – Must Watch!" (Link 4)

What is it that makes good stories capable of transcending national borders and differences?

It is the fact that even though they might involve someone far away and unfamiliar, they embody a human perspective, a statement, a point that touches the heart of every person, no matter who he or she may be.

As a consequence, when telling a story, remember that it must operate on two levels: a personal level – the part about the protagonist per se – and a universal level – the story's import, which distills the specific experiences of a given individual and thus creates an interface with humanity as a whole. If this seems obscure, it's all right: We will discuss this issue in greater detail later on.

Because a story is an excellent sales promoter.

A story is one of the best ways to promote sales. Many of us who deal in sales have known this for a long time, based

51

on our personal experience. Thus, a story we are told about a product can raise its value in our eyes tenfold or more.

This is evident in the findings of an experiment conducted by Rob Walker (Borrelli, 2012), a columnist for the *New York Times*. Walker went to a flea market and bought close to one hundred items that he describes as "insignificant," at a total cost of approximately $129, and posted them on eBay at an asking price many times higher than he had paid for them. Crucially, each item posted was accompanied by a story.

Can you guess what happened?

In the end, all the items were sold for over $3,600. This is tantamount to a 2,790 percent profit!

Can you see now the tremendous power of storytelling?

Indeed, research in consumer behavior indicates that a strong connection exists between the price customers were prepared to pay for a product and the story the salesperson had told them about it. The research found that, the better the story accompanying a product, the more the customer would pay for it and the higher the perceived value.

I have a friend who is a ceramics artist working in Jerusalem. Once, she told me that a customer of hers had found a decorated ceramic teapot to be more appealing than similar items only because the story of its creation was unusual and memorable. The customer eventually bought it at a price that was several dozen percentage points higher than that of other teapots, not less beautiful and possibly even more so.

I can attest to this phenomenon personally, based on my own experience. When I meet with a potential client, I almost always pepper our conversation with stories about my company, about the services I provide, or how I came to open my business in the first place. One of the stories that I like to tell in such meetings is this:

When I was a little girl, my favorite pastime was to

enter a store in the local shopping center and ask the salesperson for something that they clearly didn't have. For example, with a good friend holding my hand for moral support, I would go into a stationery store and in all innocence ask, "Could I please have two plain yogurts and a loaf of rye bread?" Naturally, the saleslady would look at me in wonderment, but before she could regain her senses and come up with an appropriate reply, my friend and I would be already outside, convulsing with laughter.

"Why am I telling you that?" I then ask the client, and answer this question myself: "Because if today you went, say, into a shoe store, what do you think you would be offered?" At that point, puzzled and expecting some kind of a trap, the client tentatively ventures, "Shoes?"

"Of course. When you go to a shoe store, you don't expect the salesman to say, 'Hmm, you don't need shoes, sir. What you do need is a hat!'"

And then I explain that this is precisely what I do. I am an expert to whom people come to hear what they need in terms of marketing. Because if you go to a Facebook promotion company, the staff will naturally offer to promote your services on Facebook, and if you apply to a public relations company, they will undoubtedly sell you public relations services – because that's what they do, that's how they earn their living. I, on the other hand, don't stand to gain anything by choosing one marketing platform over another; I merely offer marketing counseling and guidance, and I help businesses tell their stories. In other words, without any ulterior motive, I direct my clients to what they really need – be it a hat, a pair of shoes, or a coat – and advise them where they should invest their resources in order to get the best outcome.

When I tell the above story to my clients, they see very clearly the vantage point from which I operate. In other words, this story helps me illustrate, emphasize, and bring into focus where and how I am unique.

Reasons to engage in storytelling are many and varied, but I hope that the ones I have presented above are sufficient to convince you that invariably, when your goal vis-à-vis an audience is to touch, persuade, energize, involve, or rouse them to action, it pays to tell a story based on salient facts.

To sum up, storytelling is not a lifeless tool for transmitting information or knowledge, but first and foremost a bridge between ourselves and other people. It is a key to opening a direct channel to the hearts of others, because stories can move us; make us happy; stimulate and spur us out of inertia; frighten, oppress and disturb us; arouse anxiety; give us hope; and propel us forward – or cast us into an abyss.

Good stories can win us people's attention and consideration, because they have something that captivates the audience and keeps them in suspense: What will happen next? What is the punchline? How does it all end?

Stories render incidents meaningful and leave an impact on our consciousness; stories are important for memorizing information, for eliciting empathy and compassion, for achieving a desired interpretation and agreement, for engaging the addressee and establishing a common language.

Through framing, stories can also guide audiences to concur regarding who are "the good guys" and who are "the bad guys," what the real reason for a given outcome is and what is incidental to it, what is true and what is false, what is right and what is wrong.

Yet above all, stories are an instrument that can be used to bypass rational thought and smuggle messages under the radar, directly into the addressee's mind, whereupon they are accepted with very little resistance.

Stories make order in our reality, metaphorically speaking, and render it meaningful. They teach us about ourselves, about humankind, about life. Good, well-told stories can shape worldviews and even delimit or modify a universe of values.

Storytelling is a tool for achieving influence; it is essential for public figures, senior officials, opinion leaders, and managers. Stories, to the extent that they are properly told and constructed skillfully according to the rules, can help people in such positions gain a reputation for charisma, to establish a connection with their audiences, and to spearhead activity in their respective spheres.

Considering all this, it wouldn't be an exaggeration to say that storytelling is a highly powerful rhetorical tool par excellence. What we need to learn, then, is how to use it strategically to promote agendas, goals, and objectives as intended.

So... whether you are a leader seeking to promote a public reform, a manager who wishes to spur your employees to better performance, a lecturer who hopes to leave a mark on the hearts and minds of your listeners, a teacher trying to command your students' attention, a businessman endeavoring to present the advantages of your products or services, or a parent determined to gain your children's trust and understanding: if you wish to reach and move your audience, you must enliven your discourse with stories. And not just any stories, but ones that are solid and effective – that is to say, high-quality stories.

And now that you see why it is worth your while to tell stories – let's get to it!

But wait a minute, do we know how to tell a good story? And how can you tell what a good story is? How do we know which story to opt for – why one and not another?

7

Diversion

In order to be able to explain and demonstrate what good storytelling is all about, I would like to take you back briefly to the stories I told you about myself in the beginning of this book.

The first story recounted the events I experienced from the moment of my car accident until I opened my own company, while the second was an autobiographical summary based on the same set of facts.

Does anyone doubt that the first is much better in terms of its capacity to elicit attention and engagement? And it's also much easier to remember, isn't it? Why? What does the first story have that is missing from the second – and that makes it so much more effective?

The answer is simple: The first story I built according to the rules for creating an effective story, while the second did not follow the rules. Instead, I merely did what you have probably often heard lecturers do at the beginning of their presentations: I did this, I was that, I built, I developed, I have…

How does Jerry Seinfeld put it?
Yada, yada, yada.

Very well, then, but what are the rules for building a good story?

Before I discuss these rules – the structure, the schemas, the narrative elements, and other staples that I illustrate and elucidate in what follows – before I present guidelines for good storytelling, I would like to take the reader back to the earlier question.

What is a good story?

When, in my lectures and workshops, I put this question before the participants, the answer that I almost invariably get, especially if there are people in the audience who know something about marketing, is, "A story that sells."

"But think for a moment," I point out. "You have just stated an outcome of good storytelling, but this isn't what I asked. My question was, what makes a good story?"

At this point, usually only a few answers are voiced. For although at first glance this question sounds simple, even trivial, it is far from that.

After struggling for a while with it myself, after searching long and hard with the help of the internet, the best answer that I could come up with was: A good story is one worth telling!

OK, but what makes a story worth telling?

Well, it must be interesting for those who hear it!

No doubt you are thinking: "Please, stop beating around the bush! Let's get to the point. What makes a story interesting?"

The truth is that I haven't been able to find a comprehensive and rigorous definition, or even description, of an interesting story. Although I have sieved through a slew of versions, not one of them is good enough to do the job. Therefore, after going through this exhausting process, I decided to formulate my own definition:

A good story is content that provides a diversion.

This dictum obviously requires clarification. In this case, the term "diversion" does not imply entertainment that amuses you and makes you laugh, but is closer to the Pascalian use of this word as "distraction."

Put differently, good stories divert our minds from thinking about existence, about here and now, and transport us to a different dimension, an imaginary one.

Let us retrace our steps and try to understand how we can tell a good story, or in other words, according to my definition above, how we can communicate content in a diverting way. This will be the first step, before we deal with the question of how to use such content to get messages across.

The truth is that this is a relatively easy element in the puzzle of promoting agendas and goals through storytelling. Because telling a good story is far less complicated than you might think, especially if you use one or more of the schemas, or narrative patterns, for a successful story that I am about to demonstrate. The real difficulty will arise when we learn how to use stories to promote agendas. But we'll cross that bridge when we come to it. To begin with, I will present the schemas for effective storytelling that I have identified, starting with an explanation of the method I used to do so.

8

Methodology

When, as part of my doctoral studies, I delved into academic literature and research on discourse analysis, I learned that one of the ways to identify schemas or paradigms is by reducing a corpus of stories to their constituent elements and isolating their broadest common denominator.

You are probably wondering how this can be done.

It's not too complicated. A story is not some kind of amorphous raw material, but is comprised of discrete elements that can be isolated, separated, and further deconstructed. In other words, a story is patterned – built according to a paradigm, a blueprint. Therefore, in a process inverse to its construction, one can take a story apart into its component parts. In this way, as Shlomith Rimmon-Kenan writes in her 1984 book *Narrative Fiction: Contemporary Poetics*, one can extract a specific narrative pattern out of a story's content.

According to literary scholars, this is possible because every story resonates with a narrative paradigm prevalent in the culture or the set of communities in which that story is told. As Mikhail Bakhtin points out in his 1986 work *Speech*

Genres and Other Late Essays, although each piece of content is unique, each discipline has produced its own characteristic genres that are repeated in multiple variations.

To the extent that stories are built on a factual foundation, one can disassemble a story into its constituent narrative elements, distill its schema, and sketch out its narrative structure.

A well-known example of this strategy is found in the works of Vladmir Propp, a folklorist and scholar of the Russian formalist school, who claimed that folk tales are all essentially one and the same tale, with the sole difference among them their sets of characters and the events comprising the plot.

In other words, although the plots of various tales may include an infinite number of events and characters, the functions of these tales and the events within them are limited in number.

In the same vein, all the stories I have categorized as "good" can be distilled to a number of basic recurring schemas.

It is important to keep in mind, however, that this categorization is necessarily subjective, inasmuch as I am the one who ultimately decides which content warrants the label "good." To minimize this subjective dimension, I checked the themes identified in professional literature against those I had isolated.

Procedure

Research of this kind is premised on the notion that to identify dominant themes, various content must be juxtaposed to enable comparative reading. My purpose in comparing texts was to make it easier to detect commonalities and differences.

As a first step, I went through all the stories that I had collected and classified them into categories according to their broadest common denominator, as is usually done in qualitative comparative content analysis. Stories that fit more than one category I grouped under the rubric that, in my opinion, was the most dominant.

Juxtaposing the themes I had identified against the ones in the literature, as well as scrutinizing several texts in parallel, helped me to identify the categories and schemas within them, and to fine-tune these rubrics. Whenever I discerned a theme that was not mentioned in the literature, I created a new rubric of my own.

The stories that I examined comprised texts, images and video clips. These materials included marketing, advertising and other web content, all of which I identified as not overtly for sales purposes – which doesn't mean that they lacked an agenda.

Following this approach, on the internet in general and on social media in particular, I collected hundreds of content items that I considered to be "good." To track down the secret of their success, I pared these items down to a set of basic schemas. Throughout this process I guided myself with the following questions: Why do I judge this content to be "good"? What does it have that drives engagement? And what kinds of content (or narrative genres) strike one as more prominent and appealing?

After identifying several narrative schemas that recurred in much of the content – by consulting both my own findings and professional literature – I formulated the most common schemas for successful storytelling and sorted them into categories.

In the next chapter, I will present the main schemas for successful storytelling, under several rubrics, and whenever feasible demonstrate them using examples from the internet.

Although I have collected a vast number of examples of successful storytelling, both on the internet and from other sources, I take many of my examples from content that I myself have produced.

One reason for this choice is pragmatic: I don't have to worry about copyright issues.

The other is more substantive: When I analyze the agendas of the content discussed, using my own texts makes it easier for me to reveal the messages in the story's subtext. After all, who knows my agenda better than I?

The schemas presented here are based on paradigms that are popular, accessible, and user-friendly. This doesn't mean that other schemas do not exist; merely that they may be less widespread or more complex to analyze, unravel, and use.

And now, full steam ahead – let's get to work!

In the next chapters, I will set out the various elements that are essential for anyone who wants to build an effective story. As promised, we will start with schemas, or narrative patterns.

9

Schemas for Successful Storytelling

We live in an age saturated with messages, in which knowing how to tell a good story – one that people will want to share with others – is a must for everyone. We need to supply our audience with content that is enlightened, sophisticated, novel, exciting, enthralling, moving, entertaining, comprehensible... content that they will want to share with others, and in doing so appear informed, insightful, funny, easygoing, and abreast of things – au courant, so to speak.

As Mark Hughes put it in his 2005 book *Buzzmarketing: Get People to Talk about Your Stuff*, we need to provide our audience with currency for exchanging information – something that they can talk about, content that will bring gain to those who pass it on. And this is the key to success.

The stories that deserve to be told will always be the ones that yield perks our audience can enjoy. Such content can be delivered in a wide variety of modes, from an article or post on Facebook to a picture, video clip, or notice – but invariably it must bring the consumer some value or gain.

This could be pleasure, insight, a new angle on life, meaning, inspiration, utility, or merely diversion (in the Pascalian sense of the word), but surprisingly also anger, distress or protest. In effect, all content that has the power to evoke emotion, whether positive or negative, has the potential to become viral.

Consider for a moment. How many times have you responded to or even shared a post that aroused your antagonism or anger – possibly doing so for no other reason than to express objection or to make the point that "this is not right"? Did you stop to think that, through your action, you were effectively promulgating the objectionable post?

This is similarly the aim of all those advertisements that provoke public outrage – and thereby gain much wider exposure than they had at the outset. In such cases, every dollar invested in the original ad is multiplied tenfold, and paradoxically enough, this leverage is provided by those who objected to it in the first place. Is such virality good or bad? Well, this is a topic for another conversation.

At the core of good storytelling lies value and utility. It follows that the foundation common to all the schemas that I will set out will be to provide your audience with content that will amuse them, contribute to their knowledge, touch their hearts and minds, make them wiser, move, enthrall, infuriate, or sadden them.

If you succeed in this task, chances are that your content will engage the addressees and that they will share your stories with others. As a matter of fact, this is the principle behind virtual marketing, the method companies and businesses all over the world use to promote brands through storytelling.

Before I present the schemas that I have identified for such stories, let me explain in more detail what a schema is.

Generally speaking, a schema can be conceived of as a formula, a blueprint, a template, or a guiding principle.

However, the procedure of constructing schemas that I implemented in this research yielded patterns that are more akin to cognitive schemas.

A cognitive schema is a mechanism through which humans form a framework of expectations that helps them cope with vast amounts of information. It is a process through which we categorize into patterns information and experiences to which we are exposed in our day-to-day lives. When we encounter new or unfamiliar situations or objects, we use these paradigms to form an attitude towards these scenarios, to comprehend them, and to take a stand vis-à-vis them. For us, such schemas are essential for processing, interpreting and comprehending reality.

When reading the narrative schemas that I lay out below, you have the inverse task: You must decide which of your own stories fit into these schemas. It is important to keep in mind that the schemas presented here, on their own, are not enough to tell a successful story, so in the following chapters I will discuss other elements essential for this purpose.

Below are eight main categories I have identified, along with their respective schemas, that will give you an idea about the kind of content that has the potential to become viral and the narrative foundations they are built on:

I. Misarrangement
Resonance
Inversion

II. "Hot" Stories
News
Context
Celebrities

III. Discovery
Research
"From my own experience"

IV. Against All Odds
Cinderella
The underdog

V. "Alluring" Stories
"I have a secret!"
Scandals

VI. Mutual Responsibility
"Friends – to our aid!"
"For the good of the public"

VII. Humor
"This is really funny!"
Practical jokes

VIII. The Classic Story
The hero's journey

Under each of the above categories, with the exception of the last, more than one schema was identified, based on patterns that recurred over and over again. For stories that can fit more than one schema, I placed them under the rubric that I judged to be the most dominant.

Category I: Misarrangement

Content in this category is built on misarrangement, which can take many different forms, the classic story being rather fluid. Accordingly, I will give more than one example for this category, for the purposes of illustration and to demonstrate its diversity.

The schemas that emerged as most common here are *Resonance* and *Inversion*.

Resonance
One of the recurring schemas in this category

encompasses stories that are based on a well-known and familiar source narrative that is misarranged, often – albeit not always – to amuse the addressee.

How does it work?

It's rather simple. The story is based on a well-known narrative but, at a certain junction, the plot is twisted, resulting in the disruption of the familiar sequence of events. This misarrangement ultimately produces the desired effect. Put differently, such stories resonate, or "cite," other narratives; they engage in a dialogue with another, well-known and familiar, text. The resonance is often with trendy advertisements, popular movies or narratives that are common in a given culture or society.

Below is an example of a story created by misarranging a well-known advertisement from Israel's Government Advertising Agency, which several years ago was widely discussed in the context of sex education and condom use.

The text of the advertisement is as follows.

> "Sorry, but are you aware that, every time you sleep with your girlfriend, you also sleep with her ex-boyfriend, and with her ex-boyfriend's girlfriend, and with the boyfriend of her ex-boyfriend's girlfriend, and with the girlfriend of the boyfriend of her ex-boyfriend's girlfriend? One of you could have AIDS…"

The internet is swarming with scrambled versions of this advertisement. Here is an example.

> "Sorry, but are you aware that, every time you copy from your friend, you copy from your friend's friend, and from the friend of your friend's friend, and from the friend of the friend of your friend's friend? One of you could be a moron…"

Sometimes this platform works only when the source is well known to the target audience; otherwise, the misarrangement is not perceived as such, and the processing does not proceed as intended. In other cases, however, the message does get across, even if the addressee is unfamiliar with the source. This happens when the type of story being parodied is familiar to everyone, even if the story itself is not.

A telling example is the advertisement "Dirt Devil – The Exorcist."

For maximum effect, watch the clip before reading any further.

"Dirt Devil – The Exorcist" (Link 5)

The clip opens with a widely known episode from movie *The Exorcist*. In case you haven't seen it, it is an American horror movie produced by the Werner brothers and released at the end of 1973; it was nominated for ten Academy Awards and brought in one of the largest box-office profits in the history of cinematography. In fact, it was the first ever horror movie to be nominated for an Academy Award. I saw *The Exorcist* as a child and remember it well. Everyone talked about it, and it wouldn't be an exaggeration to say that many kids were afraid to go to sleep at night after watching it.

The advertisement uses one of the movie's prominent scenes, in which a priest, in the dark of night, enters a room where a girl is lying in bed, and she is obviously terrified. Suddenly, we become witness to a shocking spectacle. The atmosphere is eerie. The bed is shaking. The pages of a book are turning all by themselves; the door squeaks; the girl floats up from her bed towards the ceiling, and strident and horrifying screams issue from her throat. Next in the ad, the camera slowly "penetrates" the ceiling and focuses on the floor of the apartment above – and there we see a kindly, elderly lady vacuuming the carpet and humming a merry tune. At this point, the viewer realizes that the vacuum cleaner she is using is so powerful that its suction has caused everything that is happening in the apartment below.

This advertisement is an excellent example of the schema whereby a well-known story is misarranged to produce a desired effect and convey a specific meaning. In this case, even if the viewer has not seen the original film, the message gets across effectively.

Why?

Because the schema involves an easily recognizable scenario. Because most of us are familiar with some story about a demon, and this enables us to understand the context and process the contents of the clip even though we haven't seen the actual film.

Inversion

This is another schema based on misarrangement, and it is prevalent on social media. One could summarize the idea behind it as "I am going to give it to you inside out." This schema foils the addressees' expectations regarding a story that is new and unfamiliar, and the element of surprise helps achieve a desired effect.

In most cases, the story within this schema propels the audience along a certain relatively commonplace path, but at a climactic point somewhere towards the end, it deviates abruptly from the initial direction. This sharp turn takes the audience by surprise and thwarts their expectations; in other words, it undermines their predictions regarding the plot.

In contrast to the previous schema, in which the intended

purpose is often to amuse, this kind of misarrangement can be found in emotional stories that are meant to touch people's hearts. Below is a synopsis of a Facebook post based on this schema, and in this case, the intention is clearly not mere amusement.

The story is about a family man who falls in love with another woman and betrays his wife. The husband wants a divorce, but the wife won't go for it. When he tells her about his affair, she behaves strangely and refuses to give him a straightforward divorce. She is prepared to give up all her possessions, money, and other rights and privileges, on two conditions: that the husband not leave home for several weeks, and that during that time, each morning he carry her in his arms.

Thus far we cannot understand what is wrong with the woman. Why is she prepared to renounce everything – her house, the car, the money, and so on – for the benefit of an adulterous husband? Why is she asking for such an absurd thing? We have a feeling that she is grasping at straws. We pity her; her behavior seems poignant and pathetic. And then, almost at the end of the post, we discover the reason for everything: the woman is in the final stages of terminal cancer and is about to die.

This dislocation, this twist, makes the entire story meaningful and interesting. Without the ending, it is pointless and bland.

Stories that follow the inverse schema always surprise us, and this accounts for their longevity. Sometimes, this surprise element in a narrative that may otherwise be trite renders it appealing to a wide audience. It's like with some movies: At first they don't seem exciting, but then a twist in the plot makes you see the whole picture from a new perspective... and all of a sudden, you realize that the movie is not bad at all. Actually, it is quite good and well worth watching.

Misarranged stories come in a wide variety of forms.

Once you grasp the principle, however, you will be able to identify the characteristic dislocation and create stories of your own, following this pattern.

Below is another example for this schema, this time in a story of my own creation. My intention was not to amuse or move the addressee but rather to make a point about a social issue.

I've been looking for a certain pair of contact lenses for a long time now.

They are quite special. Unlike any other lenses.

Yet all my effort has been in vain: I haven't found them.

The lenses are unique, with a built-in filter akin to the one in sunglasses that eliminates radiation.

But these lenses filter out other things.

Frankly, they are the discovery of the century, comparable to the invention of the wheel. And it goes without saying that they were also created by a man.

Anyway, if one wears these lenses and looks, say, at a laundry basket, it appears empty: no laundry in it, none whatsoever. Even more bizarre, if one wants to do the wash and picks up the laundry basket while wearing the lenses, one cannot see the color of the items inside it. White and red appear the same.

Don't you think that's rather cool?

The lenses also filter out the garbage can in the bathroom. With them on, all bathroom trash becomes invisible. It is quite remarkable, really, because even if the bin is overflowing with trash, one doesn't see it! Other stuff, too – for example, if the breadbox is empty, if there is no milk in the fridge, if the shampoo is finished, and so on. But the greatest advantage of these lenses is that they filter out the toilet seat.

You are reading correctly! When you wear the

lenses, the toilet seat always appears to be in place –
it is never raised.

But do you know what's most bizarre about it
all?

Nearly all the men I know wear these lenses,
but I haven't been able to find a single pair in any
store, although I have searched everywhere.

When I asked my husband where I could find
a pair, he revealed to me, as a gesture of goodwill and
in the strictest confidence, that these lenses cannot be
purchased for money! To own a pair, he said, you
must either be born male or undergo corneal
transplant surgery, on the condition that the organ
comes from a male donor.

And here is the last example for the inverse schema, also
a post from my personal blog:

We all make a lot of mistakes, and that's OK.
Being human, we are entitled to it. We make
mistakes throughout our entire life – in choosing
what to study or what profession to join; in friendship
and in love; in marriage and about our children's
education… We make dozens, hundreds, thousands
of mistakes.

Yet, there is one kind of mistake that we
absolutely cannot afford to make: We cannot make
wrong decisions about anything that has to do with
our children's health.

For example, if a child was running a very high
temperature and her mother failed to give her fever-
reducing medication, what would you say? And what
would be your reaction if I told you that the child
subsequently lost consciousness and developed
convulsions? And what would you say if I told you
that, in this case, the mother managed to make the

maximum number of mistakes in the shortest possible time? What would you think about that mother if I told you that the child had to be taken to the nearest hospital by ambulance?

Well, I know what I would have to say about such a mother. I would say she is a criminal. I would add that, for this kind of negligence, she should be behind bars! This is what I really believe – and if it were at all possible, I would give myself up to the police.

As I explained above, what all the narratives in this category have in common is that they lead the audience along a certain route and, at some critical point, thwart their expectations.

Category II: "Hot" Stories

This category encompasses content that is presented as novel, nifty or, trendy, or that concerns an issue that is currently on the public agenda, or a person who happens to be at the center of public attention.

The three most common schemas in this category are termed here as *News*, *Context*, and *Celebrities*.

News

When I was studying for an MA in communication and journalism at the Hebrew University, one of the most common definitions of "news" went like this: if a dog bites a man – it's not news; if a man bites a dog – it's news.

So if you have stories with a novel element, they are likely to arouse interest. In such a case, your story can easily translate from the internet to traditional media outlets. Today, when most of us have a camera and video recorder in our pockets, the chance to witness and document something memorable and thus attain our five minutes of glory is much greater than ever before.

Context

However, most of us will not in all probability get to generate news. And this is the advantage of the context schema: It capitalizes not on something that is in itself novel, but rather on something that interfaces with a novelty, in the sense of a subject that is already present on the public agenda or marked on the calendar, whether of a local, national, or international scope.

Below is an example of a post that I wrote based on the context schema and where I reference an issue discussed on the news.

When I worked as a spokeswoman, I was asked by the regional director to draw journalistic focus to an ancient and decrepit bridge in some remote rural area in Israel.

Despite my efforts, not a single journalist had expressed any interest in this structure. After all, in a country like ours, rife with terror attacks, wars, and other disasters that compete for headlines along with other problems vital to our day-to-day existence, most of them immensely complex, and where "hot news" oozes out of every crack and crevice, what chance is there that anyone would care about an ancient bridge located far away from any metropolitan center?

Except...

Around that time, the Maccabiah catastrophe happened. On July 14, 1997, during the opening ceremony of the 15th Maccabiah Games, a pedestrian bridge collapsed over the Yarkon River in Tel Aviv, killing four Australian athletes and injuring sixty more. As soon as the disaster hit the headlines, my similarly godforsaken bridge was a big deal. Suddenly, every single journalist was tripping over themselves to produce an item about that ramshackle and "worthless" structure.

In this unarguably disgraceful and deplorable case, the temporal proximity between the collapse and my efforts to draw attention to my bridge linked them together, without any extra effort on my part. However, the context schema is relevant not only when negative news is concerned and not only at the national level. Let me elaborate: When you give a lecture or upload a post or an article, it pays to include a story that interfaces with something that is currently "hot news"; if your story is contextually linked with such news, this is the time to tell it, whether on the internet or to a live audience.

Why?

Because people tend to consume content in context. Often it is the context that makes a story interesting, as in the above example of the bridge. This is why we should take into consideration the context of a story. It may be salient to one person but not to another. For example, if a sick person sees a story about someone who has a similar illness, that person will find the story interesting.

Contextual factors vary in the scope of their salience. They can operate:

- at the international level; for example, stories about women recounted on International Women's Day;
- at the national level; for example, stories related to national holidays;
- at the local level; for example, stories about regional events.

Here is an example of an association that I made in a routine post that elicited engagement and was shared by viewers, exponentially increasing sales of my book as part of a fundraising campaign to enable its publication. In a matter of several hours, the post raised over a thousand dollars for the project, without my lifting a finger!

At that time, it was reported on the news that the Israeli Education Ministry had banned Dorit Rabinian's novel *All the Rivers*. I immediately uploaded the following post.

Every Saturday morning, at 9 o'clock precisely, my father calls me on the phone. It's been like that for years. We live far away from each other, and interact mostly over the phone. Usually we chat for half an hour or so, filling each other in on what happened during the past week.

Today my father asked me how my book has been selling online. "Nothing to boast about," I replied. "Why?" he inquired. "Aren't you promoting it?" "As a matter of fact, yes, I am," says I. "My Facebook posts get quite a bit of engagement and dozens of 'shares' and 'likes,' and so too my WhatsApp messages – everyone's been so supportive..." "And how many orders have you got?" he persisted. "Well, actually very few," I answered awkwardly. "Two from very close relatives, one from a childhood friend who is also a client, one from a good friend, one from my former boss who has always believed in me, one from my mom's friend, one from my current client, and one from someone who is very well known in Israel as a life coach."

"So how would you explain such a lack of interest?" he asked. "It's very simple," I said. "I still haven't reached my target audience. This is the ABC of marketing. It doesn't matter how much effort I am putting into promotion; unless I get to my target audience – those for whom the book was written in the first place, whom it will impact, whose needs it addresses, or those who want to take part in its success – all the promotion is for nothing."

My father, who is a very smart person even if his interests do not include marketing, immediately retorted, "Nonsense. What you really need is for the Education Ministry to ban your book."

So where do you come in, in this story? How can you help?

1. If you are among my target audience and would like to order the book, you can do so at the following link: http://www...

2. You can arrange for my book to be banned by the Education Ministry, the Finance Ministry, Prime Minister's Office, or any other official body even before it is published.

3. You can share this post.

4. You can do all of the above, or part thereof.

5. You can tell me: "Give yourself a break, Osnat! What do you need all that headache for? It would be better for everyone if you just forgot about it."

So which option do you choose?

Just remember that a story is always embedded in a context, and it pays to find an opening to tap into it. The context that increases the salience of a story at the ideational level can be genuine, but it can also be only a gimmick, as in my post cited above.

Celebrities

Stories in this schema are about people who are in the limelight, to a greater or lesser extent, in the sense that they are the focus of public attention. This may rightly strike you as bordering on trivial. We are talking here about any celebrity, from the ones coughed up by reality shows – such as *Big Brother, Survivor,* or *MasterChef* – to businesspeople, politicians, or millionaires who have gained either fame or notoriety by virtue of their own qualities, their families, or good luck.

People love to hear about the lives of others in general, but especially the rich, the famous, the beautiful, and the successful. Therefore, any story about a celebrity, a mini-celebrity, or a quasi-celebrity captivates the general public.

We can safely assume that this propensity stems from a natural voyeuristic impulse, a desire to gain a glimpse of other people's lives, which can be motivated by adoration, jealousy, the joy of gloating, our hope that maybe some of their glamour will rub off on us, or simply our copycat tendencies. Peeking through a peephole, as it were, fulfils a variety of needs, but often makes us feel that we are part of it all – or at least that we appear that way to others.

An example isn't even necessary here. Just go on the internet, and in no time at all you will find scores of such stories.

Category III: Discovery

This category contains content that lures us in by promising to teach us something we don't know. It may profess to offer new insights into human nature, social behavior, or other people's experiences.

The two most prominent schemas here are *Research* and *"From my own experience."*

Research

Much of our conduct in life is guided by common sense, by what we have learned from others, and by what we have learned from personal experience or by observing our surroundings, as well as by our feelings and beliefs. Yet often we feel that we are groping in the dark, trying to choose between mutually contradictory courses of action or conflicting theories, or deliberating whether to act according to our own or other people's experience. What is right? What is wrong?

Research can provide us with answers to such dilemmas. It may suggest ways to resolve cognitive dissonance, as well as an escape route out of misgivings and doubts. Should I or shouldn't I vaccinate my children against papilloma? Is coffee good or bad for my health?

It's not only studies about health issues that provide this kind of insight, but also research or surveys that explain something about our world, ourselves, human nature, socialization processes, where we stand in relation to other people – about life in general.

When research findings and survey data are presented in the form of stories rather than as a conglomeration of facts, they have the potential to either endorse or refute beliefs, to suggest a useful behavioral strategy, to help us make some order in the chaos and clutter of our lives, to mark a path for us... Such possibilities render research a viable schema for a successful story.

And now you are in for a surprise. Under this narrative rubric is also found a lot of pseudo-research, that is, studies that are not based on the established scientific method, like the ones conducted in accredited research institutes worldwide. And in spite of this, such stories can be effective. Even stories that their authors themselves label as self-study or market research, even a perfunctory comparison between two products or services, even insights presented as scientific but bearing only a remote resemblance to science: such stories, too, succeed in beguiling a wide variety of audiences.

Below are two popular advertisements that use this schema.

The first promotes Beldent chewing gum. It presents an experiment in which the Beldent company endeavors to gauge people's beliefs and perceptions regarding gum chewing, for no other purpose than to topple the social stigma attached to this behavior. The clip features several pairs of identical twins, one of whom chews gum and the other of whom doesn't, this being the only difference between them. Needless to say, the brand of gum used in the ad is Beldent.

The participants, all members of the general public, come

to the laboratory, receive a pair of earphones, and are asked to answer some questions by way of pressing buttons.

For example, a participant is seated facing a pair of identical twins, both wearing a police uniform, one chewing gum and the other not. The participant is asked through the earphones, which one is the bad cop? Which one will enjoy giving you a ticket? And so on.

Can you guess the results?

"Beldent Almost Identical" (Link 6)

In the second advertisement, which promotes the Always brand, the "research" element is less prominent than, or at least not as overt as, in the previous one, but the viewer still gets the impression that some kind of research or science is involved. By tapping into a value central to its target audience, women, the advertisement is designed to undermine the derisive attitude and negativity associated with the turn of speech "like a girl," as in "You throw like a girl," "You fight like a girl." The ad manages to present quasi-science as credible research documenting participants' responses in real time. The result is a good story that impresses, moves, and engages the viewer.

"Always #LikeAGirl" (Link 7)

I would like to stress at this point that the materials that I use in this book to demonstrate successful storytelling are not intended to serve as examples of good sales outcomes. All the patterns I present here constitute schemas for successful storytelling, but at no point do I presume to suggest that any of this has been translated to financial gain.

The main reason for this qualification is that I don't have data regarding the story's aim in every given case, and this aspect can vary widely and does not necessarily relate to sales. Nor do I have any information about the monetary success of these campaigns. There is no one I know who could share with me the relevant data, and even if I had such an opportunity, I wouldn't be able to tell whether it was accurate.

When I designate a story as successful, my judgment relates only to its constituent elements, its popularity among audiences, and its capacity to elicit interest and engagement. There is no implication whatsoever that a good narrative necessarily translates to profit.

Here is another, albeit totally different, example, this time a text that I wrote while faithfully following the research schema. Note that here I go one step further, though I do not claim or even allude to scientific validity or a solid evidence base. This is because I never actually researched the issue, in the normative sense of this word; in fact, I explicitly state that the survey I describe cannot by any stretch of the imagination be considered representative.

A few days ago I came face to face with a weird phenomenon. A weird male phenomenon.

Or at least, this is what I naïvely thought.

Today, after spending every minute of my scarce free time conducting a biased and unrepresentative survey, I realized that the phenomenon I am talking about is rather widespread. I was perplexed with the results of my research (and also quite angry at myself for yet again wasting my best leisure hours on a stupid study).

Be that as it may, this time the issue I investigated was whether men know how to braid hair.

What made me study this absurd subject?

An encounter with the father of two daughters, in which he asked me to help braid the older one's hair.

"Why can't you do it yourself?" I inquired rather vociferously.

"Because I have no idea how to do it!" he shamelessly replied.

I must mention here that I know this individual personally and can thus testify that his mental abilities are all in order. He is in his thirties and has an advanced academic degree in a prestigious scientific field. For all that, he has no idea how to make a braid. "What does that have to do with anything?" he squawked when I laid out the paradox before him.

Anyway, my findings unambiguously show that men don't know how to braid hair. Full stop.

My research sample comprised 10 fathers with at least one daughter each, and not one of them was able to make a braid.

I don't know what results I would have

obtained had I studied men in general rather than only fathers of girls, but even though I am not very good with numbers (though I am quite competent at recognizing zeros), I realize that, in this case, a negative result is out of the question.

So I will ask you now: How is it possible that men are capable of accomplishing such complex tasks as designing an airplane or inventing the atomic bomb, but when it comes to simple things like braiding some hair or separating dirty laundry into colors and whites, they get all mixed up?

It's not because they don't usually have ten fingers on their hands or are colorblind.

Believe me, these assumptions I have already tested.

"From my own experience"

This schema includes all the stories in the corpus in which people talk about treatments, medications, foods, other people, incidents, and so on that have helped them overcome an illness, a problem, or pain, or that have changed, impacted, or saved their own or other people's lives, and other similar scenarios. As in the previous schema, stories under this rubric help us make decisions when we are in doubt about what's good for us or how to change our way of life. They encourage us to learn from other people's experience to cope with problems or to get to know others who are going through the same kind of suffering as we are and to learn hope from them – that there is a way out of the ostensible impasse and that it only needs to be found, studied, and followed.

This schema is widespread in social media, and good stories get a lot of responses. I don't think examples are necessary here, either: Just log into social media, and you will find them everywhere, like ants at a picnic.

Category IV: Against all odds

This category contains stories in which the plot epitomizes the expression "against all odds." It includes two main schemas, which for all intents and purposes dovetail into one, but which I have decided to keep separate on account of the different conventions of schema-based genres.

As the following discussion shows, the rate at which each of these schemas is used is contingent on the purpose for which it is enlisted. The first would be appropriate for a story about an individual who surmounts personal limitations or those imposed by their surroundings or society, while the second is more salient when an individual or a group faces and overcomes some rival force, as in a head-on battle.

These two schemas are termed here *Cinderella* and *The underdog*.

Cinderella

Once my mother told me: "No matter what happens, don't ever take hope away from another person." The Cinderella schema is anchored in precisely this principle – hope. It taps into every person's deep yearning, the belief that everything is possible, everything is within our reach.

According to this schema, every one of us as individuals can be transformed from a disheveled charwoman into a beauty; from an ugly duckling shunned by all humanity to a noble swan, glamorous and sought after; from a green, slimy frog to a prince on a white horse; from a bedraggled, loud-mouthed hussy to a fine lady....

Many business success stories rest on this platform. In most of them, the protagonist prevails over all the obstacles placed before them and against all odds attains success, often on a grand scale. A story of this kind can be about a jobless person whom the unemployment office sends to a chocolate-making course and who subsequently opens a shop and before long expands overseas; or about someone who barely knows how to read and write, a school dropout with no higher education, who against all odds starts a company and floats it on the stock market; or about a single mother, possibly unemployed, who becomes a world-famous author; or about a desperate housewife who becomes the owner of a prosperous business with a six-digit annual turnover.

These and similar tales are predicated on the Cinderella schema and are extremely widespread in business journalism, so much so that some people have even claimed that the messages conveyed through such stories are designed to endorse the capitalist regime.

Be that as it may, the popularity of this schema cannot be exaggerated – insofar as it is used correctly, of course – because such stories epitomize events and experiences, however fantastic and preposterous, that none of us would refute. In fact, whether openly or secretly, we all long for these dreams to come true for us as well. If such a thing happened to you, it can also happen to me. This schema is the apotheosis of hope.

The underdog

Stories that show how the weak overpower their stronger rivals are classic examples of the "Against all odds" category. These are the "few against many" stories and other equally implausible tales in which, contrary to all expectations, an underdog gains the upper hand over their bitterest enemies.

Think about the most exciting stories you know or the great myths you may have heard. Recall David, small in stature and armed with only a sling, facing the giant Goliath decked in shining armor; a scrappy band of Jedi knights attempting to take down a galaxy-wide evil institution; activist Erin Brockovich going up against a utility behemoth in court without even a law degree…. These are just some of the hundreds of stories based on this popular schema.

Category V: Alluring Stories

The common denominator among the wide variety of stories under this rubric involves "the forbidden," in the sense of something that one is not supposed to talk about. Alternatively, such stories can be about a subject that one is allowed to discuss but is considered "improper." Yet other stories are about something that one would like to know about, but is either unknown or is not supposed to be mentioned by virtue of public consensus – or anything else that may give rise to controversy or scandal. Anything that is "not subject to discussion" evokes curiosity and as such is perfect material for successful storytelling.

The main schemas identified in this category are *"I have a secret!"* and *Scandals*.

"I have a secret!"

This can be information that only the chosen few possess, which gives them power over others. We know something that others don't. We are in on a secret; we have a secret recipe. As soon as we announce that we are going to reveal a secret, we arouse our addressees' curiosity, interest, and attention. It is not a coincidence that the internet is rife with content whose titles contain the word "secrets." In fact, a marketing study showed that emails bearing such titles were opened at a greater rate than others.

Scandals

In this schema, the scandals revolve mostly around "sex, lies, and videotape."

They usually involve the bedroom and are a proven recipe for successful storytelling, possibly because they give us a glimpse into other people's lives and thus satisfy our voyeuristic tendencies, akin to soap operas. Often, they also show us that reality can be more entertaining than fiction.

At times, such stories are about the extramarital

dalliances of presidents and heads of state, often known for many years but never publicly discussed. Once this information leaks out, however, it spreads like fire in straw and enlivens the routine that makes up our existence – well, at least for most of us, and at least on the surface of things. Recall, for example, Bill Clinton's affair with Monica Lewinsky. This case alone attests to the immense power and possible repercussions of such stories.

However, scandals need not involve public figures or celebrities: a glimpse into the sex lives of neighbors or friends serves the purpose equally well, as do stories about lies, "hot" recordings, or adulterous spouses.

Category VI: Mutual Responsibility

Included under this rubric are stories that contain a personal narrative of a sensitive nature that in most cases also exposes the narrator's vulnerable points. Such sharing of confidences is usually designed to elicit the empathy, acknowledgment, and support of the target audience. Most stories of this kind do indeed win readers' sympathy and involvement by virtue of their emotional element, which is dominant in this schema in general.

The two main schemas I identified in this category are *"Friends – to our aid!"* and *"For the good of the public."*

"Friends – to our aid!"

In his 1997 book *Story*, Robert McKee said that emotion is the fast lane to the brain. In a similar vein, the third rule of wizardry cited in one of my eldest daughter's fantasy books is "Passion rules reason."

To the extent that emotional stories have the power to bypass logical reasoning and dodge people's objections, they can be used to mobilize massive support for an ideology, a business, or a project.

In this category, the narrator shares with the public a

personal story, which is often but not always a difficult one, and afterwards asks them to purchase, endorse, promote, or recommend the narrator's services (or those of a friend or a close associate) in order to help them find a way out of a distressing situation, an impasse, or a difficulty of any sort.

Occasionally, seeking what is often called "the wisdom of the crowd," the narrator asks for advice or recommendation, for example, regarding the design of her book cover or a company logo. Alternatively, a business owner may appeal to the public to buy his products or services to get out of a crisis. He is not asking for favors or charity, mind you, but rather invokes mutual responsibility. Or it may be a person who has a dream and needs help to realize it, either in return for goods or services, or for gratitude alone.

Stories that follow this schema are often about publicly funded projects on Kickstarter and the like. They can be about a singer who wants to return to the stage, a group of young people who want to make a movie, a writer who wants to publish his first book, a sick child who requires expensive treatment overseas, and so on and so forth.

"For the good of the public"

The internet is full of stories built according to this schema, and they vary in purpose and design. Such stories may contain warnings against something or someone, or they may update us on developments we should have followed but may have missed. They may inform us about a representative action that could win us money, about a governmental decision that could affect us in one way or another, about a pernicious computer program that invades and appropriates our bank accounts, about a destructive decision of Facebook's management that impinges on our privacy, and much more. Stories of this kind are prone to become viral because people's first impulse is to share and publicize them, and thereby benefit the public – even though a lot of them are totally fictional.

Category VII: Humor

This category is simple and straightforward; it includes all content that amuses us and elicits our laughter, both benign and malicious.

The two main schemas under this headline are *"This is really funny!"* and *Practical jokes*.

"This is really funny!"

People love to be amused. Funny stories and jokes of any size and color always get the floor, and they are inherently viral. And not only jokes but all kinds of allusion, dirty innuendo, bathroom tales, "smelly tales" – yes, yes, everything to do with shitting and farting. These kinds of stories engender laughter mixed with discomfiture, and they are highly contagious.

Have you ever asked yourself why practical jokes are so viral, why people are so eager to tell others about something hilarious that they have heard or experienced – why we trip over ourselves to share anything that is funny and entertaining? Well, it's simple enough: Funny stuff does not, for the most part, evoke opposition or give rise to controversy (with the exception of black humor and racist jokes, for example), and neither does it require deep thought or much mental effort. Besides, not only do we love a good laugh, but we also want to be defined as having a sense of humor and as funny. And in general, making another person laugh is seen as a good deed.

I don't include here any examples of the jokes, pictures, or clips that circulate in the various enclaves of the internet. To find numerous examples of these, all you need to do is open WhatsApp. I will, however, exemplify this schema through anecdotes, innuendos, and self-deprecating humor, stories whose intention is to make us smile. These align with the schema in this case, even if they are meant to elicit nothing more than a giggle. The reason I place these stories under the rubric of "humor" is their purpose, which is to bring a smile to our lips, even if it comes at the expense of the addressee or the raconteur themselves.

Here is an example from my personal blog.

I don't remember any of my friends with children ever mentioning this.

Definitely not.

I am sure I am right.

To avoid accusations that I haven't tried to warn you all, I am offering an advance warning. So that, when you have kids, you will be ready. So that it will not hit you out of the blue, as happened to me. Here it is.

Invariably, in every Hollywood movie, there is a point where a breathtakingly handsome main character finds a safe refuge. A place to which he flees in order to unwind and recharge his batteries – whereupon, thus fortified, he feels ready to face and cross swords with all the world's evil, the second time around. The same privilege is conferred on the female protagonist, who is likewise breathtakingly beautiful (this goes without saying). To her, as well, the movie apportions amazing places of refuge – seashore cliffs, hidden groves on the banks of mighty streams, and so on. There she resolves the affairs of the heart (because what other problems can one expect breathtaking beauties to have?).

Let's face it, we all have such a place. A private refuge of our own. Sometimes it's picturesque, like in the movies, and sometimes a little less so, such as a backyard garden, a thicket behind your apartment block, or even the local coffee house. Whatever it may be, this is where we retire for a little while to emerge refreshed and ready to deal with the vicissitudes of life.

However, when children enter the picture, everything changes. Our place of refuge becomes subject to a set of strict rules. First, it must be inside the house, and second, it must be private. And it must be completely clear to your spouse and kids that any intrusion has to be justified. And the justification had better be very convincing!

And so it happens that the bathroom becomes a place of refuge par excellence.

Think about it – it's not for nothing that a lavatory is also called a "commode" or a "comfort station." When there are toddlers in the house, the toilet becomes the most convenient private space you could envision. Even the act of expurgation (the term deriving from purging, or cleansing) attests to the true purpose of the lavatory. It is a place where we purge ourselves of everything extraneous, to which we flee to cleanse our bodies and souls of all the mess and racket of the household and the kids.

The upshot is that the bathroom is the most important place in our home. It's where we stash newspapers, books, magazines, lists of things to do, and so on. Believe me, if it weren't so disgusting, we would put the coffee machine there as well.

So if you are planning the home of your dreams, take into consideration what I have just told you, and make sure that your bathroom is large enough to hold all the things that a place of refuge must have.

By way of another example, you can watch an IKEA clip at the link below. It is pleasant and hilarious all at once. The question is, of course, at whose expense?

Watch and you'll find out.

"Experience the Power of a Bookbook"
(Link 8)

In my opinion, this IKEA clip is simply wonderful. It ridicules Apple in a subtle and sophisticated manner, but also makes fun of us, end users – and causes us to fall in love with the clip itself, although for all intents and purposes, it is only an advertisement.

However, under this schema we can also find malicious laughter, in the form of black humor, sarcasm, and the like – the kind of humor that forces our society or parts thereof to look at itself in the mirror.

Read, for example, the following passage.

Seeking a good-looking bachelor, thirty-plus, tall, with a sense of humor, intelligent, and educated. Must be respectably and gainfully employed. Preferably with a fat bank account. Not stingy and prepared to indulge a woman. Must not root for any soccer team. Consumes alcohol in moderation and smokes no more than one cigarette over twenty-four hours. Must own a house or at least an apartment. Must be mature for his age and attentive to a woman's needs. Sensitive and smart. Well-built, preferably with a magnificent physique yet not overly muscular. Gentle and considerate. Must have good taste in clothing and know how to gain the favor of a single woman's mother. No hair on his back, shoulder blades, shoulders, buttocks... and a few other places. No hair sticking out of nostrils or ears. Must have personal charm and charisma – a lot of both! Faithful like a dog and independent like a cat. Ready and able to commit to a long-term monogamous relationship. Must have a saintly mother who will make an amazing grandmother when the time comes....

What, is he not here yet?

Ugh, that's a pity.

Oh well, we'll survive.

I forgot to mention that the above list was compiled by a lady who is single-minded, determined, and not easily daunted – she won't give up. If she has set a goal for herself, she will get there someday. Give her another year or two, or maybe another twenty years... and then what? She will stand her ground, no matter what.

And come to think about it: Why would I want to discourage her? Why am I meddling at all? What do I know? How can I even think of wrecking her hope?

Clearly, there is such a man! Clearly, he will choose her and her alone!

And here is the last example, this time based on self-deprecating humor, in which advertising and marketing people ridicule the industry they work in and things they have to do to produce a successful advertisement – all the tricks and secrets of their trade.

"Jennifer Aniston Goes Viral for Smartwater"
(Link 9)

Practical jokes

Who doesn't like practical jokes? There is something quite amusing about practical jokes. If we try to understand what practical jokes are really about and why they work, we will discover that their secret lies in breaking the mold. Such an effect is achieved when we are exposed to something unexpected, often diametrically opposite to the initial scenario. Think, for example, of a ceremonial occasion, with a head of state in attendance and everyone on their best behavior – formal, solemn, and subdued – and all of a sudden, someone stumbles or, god help us, farts.

A practical joke uncovers our common denominator by showing that we are all basically made of the same stuff, and only the dramas, comedies, and vaudevilles that we act out on the stage of life make us different from one another. In this sense, a practical joke can be construed as a wink at the play itself, at the theatrical conventions that it follows, and at the ego games that we all engage in. Put differently, a practical joke reminds us not to take ourselves too seriously.

One of the most successful practical jokes authored by a business was devised by the Pepsi Corporation. Use the link below to watch it before reading on.

"Pepsi MAX & Jeff Gordon Present: 'Test Drive'" *(Link 10)*

What is amazing about this practical-joke story is not that it became viral: that would have been expected. What happened was that a TV journalist became skeptical that the clip was genuine and came up with all kinds of "proof" that the whole thing had been fabricated. However, what he actually did was help Pepsi get a slam-dunk. Pepsi then took advantage of the situation and immediately put out a sequel to the first clip, in which the butt of the joke was none other than the journalist himself.

The new clip operates according to another schema, the one where a text interfaces with a "hot" topic that is already present on the journalistic agenda – in this case, owing to the labors of the very same journalist.

Category VIII: The Classic Story

This category includes one schema, which is likewise archetypal: *The hero's journey.*

The hero's journey

This schema can be plausibly regarded as a prototype for numerous sub-patterns. It is one of the most common story templates in general, and its narrative structure often serves as part of the other schemas discussed in this book. Simply put, this paradigm can and often does coexist with others.

The hero's journey schema is based on Aristotle's theory in which the narrator must lead the hero towards a certain goal, the path to which must be strewn with obstacles, hazards, and other difficulties in order to stir the audience's emotions and cause them to identify with that hero. This kind of identification, according to the theory, will make the audience feel concerned and anxious about the hero's fate and empathize with him in all his tribulations. When the hero overcomes an obstacle or escapes danger, we feel relieved; the tension subsides, and we experience what Aristotle termed "catharsis."

In line with this theory, we can define stages through which we need to lead our audience in order to produce a "good" story within this schema.

Sympathy with the hero – This is achieved by outlining the various obstacles the hero is about to face (exposition). These can involve another individual, nature, the hero himself, society, and more.

Concern about the hero's fate – All the tribulations that befall the hero (peripeteia) make the audience commiserate with him, identify with his distress, and fear for his safety.

Catharsis – When the hero resolves a complicated situation or surmounts an obstacle (denouement), the audience feels a release of tension. It is noteworthy that, contrary to a common belief, resolving a problem does not necessarily entail a happy ending. Often, it comes as an insight, a lesson learned, or a message derived from the story.

Below is an excellent example of the hero's journey in a clip created by the Audi company:

"Audi R8 Big Game Commercial – Commander"
(Link 11)

This story demonstrates clearly the use of this schema. An astronaut (the hero) has lost the will to live (complication): he doesn't eat or talk to other people, and is indifferent to his surroundings. The solution comes in the form of an R8 Audi vehicle, which he receives as a present from his son and which restores his interest in life. It is important to track the path the authors follow to advance their agenda: the car is made to resemble a spaceship; the soundtrack uses wonderful music by David Bowie; the clip itself was released shortly after the composer's death, thereby achieving powerful extra-textual contextualization and a very strong contextual link; the vehicle is traveling towards the moon; the voices of America at its best fill every frame. The overall message is that, for Audi R8, even the sky is not the limit.

Below is another example of a clip that aligns with the hero's journey schema, and here the plot doesn't even incorporate the product. The clip is about Budweiser's puppy:

"Budweiser: Super Bowl XLVIII Puppy Love #BudEpicAds" (Link 12)

I must stress once again that the hero's journey pattern may not warrant a designation as a separate schema or category, but can rather be construed as a possible narrative structure that can be implemented in many of the stories in our corpus. For all that, its prevalence in business storytelling induced me to define it as a separate category and schema. For the same reason, I think it needs to be rendered comprehensible and accessible to anyone who wishes to use it to promote either their own business or an organization they work for.

Thus, for example, this schema is often favored by therapists, who tell their clients about a problem or an illness, either their own or a family member's, or about a friend who prompted them to embark on a search for a solution, which they eventually found in the form of a certain service or product. The rationale is that, by putting themselves in their client's place, the therapist communicates to the latter that they, too, have experienced the same problem and eventually found a way out of the impasse. This message is effectively conveyed through a personal story, which is accepted and internalized inasmuch as there is no need to overcome the mistrust, cynicism, and resistance that overt advertising might have engendered.

That's it, as far as the schemas are concerned. I have presented to you all the prominent recurring schemas that I have identified in the corpus.

And now that we have learned the main schemas for successful storytelling, are we ready to use them to build stories that will captivate our audiences?

The answer is no.

Well, it is at this point. To engage in successful storytelling, it is not enough to create a story platform using a common schema; we need something else as well: namely, the constituent elements of the story or the basic units of narrative, which the professional literature calls narrative or textual qualities.

However, before I explain what these elements are, I must introduce a component that is necessary in any story built according to the schemas for successful storytelling.

10

Structural Framework

In presenting the constituent elements of the story, I will rely on the structural framework set out by William Labov in his 1972 book *Language in the Inner City*.

Those of you who would like a basic checklist, a road map, as a tool to help build a story based on successful schemas and in line with narrative rules are invited to use these elements as mileposts.

Below are brief explanations of each of these six components (abstract, orientation, complication, evaluation, resolution, and coda), adjusted and fine-tuned to serve our purposes.

Abstract

This is basically an overview of the story. This part answers the question, "What is the story about?"

Orientation

In the journalistic jargon, orientation is sometimes termed "the five Ws." These are contextual clues that establish the referential framework of the story. The questions answered in this part are Who? What? Where? When? Why?

Complication

This element constitutes a conundrum, a problem, an obstacle, or a precipitating event. The question that is answered here is, "What happened?"

Bruner (1991) posited that a narrative must breach or deviate from an implicit canonical script in a manner that does violence to the latter's legitimacy. This discrepancy between what is anticipated and what actually occurs drives the story's dialectic movement. The emphasis is naturally on the unexpected. It follows that, for a story to be worthy of being told, it has to pivot on an episode that substantively changes the predictable flow of events. I would add here that such an event must be significant to the characters, so that we can distinguish between a routine occurrence and an extraordinary one that brings about a change in the status quo.

Without an evil character, a complication, a problem, or a dislocation of some sort, we will not be able to tell an effective story. Thus, every story we build must incorporate some sort of entanglement in the plot, in the sense of an occurrence that gives rise either to a difficulty or to a novel or unexpected scenario.

If you go back to the examples of schemas for successful storytelling that I presented earlier, or even to my personal stories in the opening chapter of this book, you will realize that all of them, without exception, include an element of complication. It takes the form of either an isolated problem or obstacle, or a sequence of hardships or impediments that the protagonist encounters along the way.

Do you remember the Aristotelian theory of narrative? And the "hero's journey" schema?

A dilemma, a complication, or an unexpected occurrence – these are among the central attributes of a story that is worth being told.

Think about the Titanic: If not for that iceberg, it would have gone down in history as just another luxury ocean liner, and nothing else. Nice, but no more than that. Accordingly, it is vital that we know how to include in our story a difficulty, a shift, or an incident that will serve as its fundamental turning point – which is true for any story. This is the point where the plot begins to unfold, a trigger that propels the story forward, but at the same time a force that molds the characters according to their responses to the evolving situation.

Evaluation

Note that evaluation is a story component that is not restricted to a specific part of the text. It is a set of tools or means that are interspersed throughout the entire story. The question that is answered by this category concerns the author's stance vis-à-vis the events narrated. Thus evaluation gives some indication of the significance the author assigns to their story and of their purpose in telling it.

Evaluation tools are essentially building materials the narrator uses to propel the story and audience to a desired destination. Evaluation is manifested in the way the story elements are arranged and in the use of rhetorical means to guide the addressees to adopt the narrator's perspective on what is being told. This component – which, as Labov himself stresses, is the most important in a story – requires in-depth discussion and will be discussed at length in the chapter devoted to promoting agendas through storytelling.

Resolution

This is where the complication is untangled. The salient question here is, "And what happened then?"

This component describes the outcome of the way the protagonist deals with the difficulties that they have encountered. In this part of our story, we need to recount the protagonist's attempts to overcome the obstacles or to solve the problem presented in the complication.

Does it mean that the story must have a happy ending?

No, it does not. Because the resolution teaches the audience what should have happened, what would have been the right thing to do, and how the complication was eventually resolved. This does not imply that the problem was dealt with in the best possible way or even constructively.

In a story, the outcome need not be positive insofar as the protagonist is concerned; he may have failed to overcome the barrier or been defeated; alternatively, she may have surmounted the obstacle – but the way she did so could have been wrong. Plotted on the success-failure axis, all these possibilities can constitute the final outcome.

In the event that the protagonist of our story has failed to resolve the problem, or if they did overcome it but went about it in a counterproductive way, the audience can learn a lesson about what not to do. The solution, in this case, serves as a vehicle for learning. We must therefore remember that, without an outcome, if only the problem is presented, there is no story as such. The narrative lacks a point, and the essence of the story is lost.

Coda

In line with Labov's theory, the coda signals that the story has ended and returns the listener to the here and now of the real world. For our purposes, I will augment the scope of this component by logically extending Labov's explicit definition, and describe it as the main point of the story. Because this is how I understand a story's main point – a reversal in the old order or the creation of a new one. Accordingly, the important question for this component is, "What lesson(s) can I learn from the story?"

Those are the components of a story in light of the general

framework of Labov's theory.

Let's assume that I have managed to convince you that storytelling pays off. We will also assume that you understand how helpful the use of schemas for successful storytelling can be in building effective stories, that you are going to implement Labov's components in building a story within a schema of your choice, and that you have enough know-how to do this.

But at this point I will raise my hand and say – wait.

Please, stop!

Before you roll up your sleeves and get to work...

Pouring content components into the cast of a schema for successful storytelling will certainly get you started – but it is not enough to keep you on the right track. To make your stories effective, it is not enough to set them into one or another popular template and put the components together – stories must incorporate several additional crucial elements.

So what are these narrative qualities without which storytelling cannot achieve the desired effect?

11

Narrative Qualities

Narrative qualities are the narrative staples, or proto-elements, that we must add to the content of our stories. Otherwise, they would be devoid of substance, and we would probably fail to achieve our goals.

It would not be an exaggeration to say that these elements are essential to effective storytelling. Incorporating them will ensure that your content has its intended effect. Well, almost. Later on, you will need to add a pinch of what I call "seasoning." But first – the staples.

In successful storytelling, these narrative proto-elements resonate with the statements in McKee's book *Story*. Following the rationale developed in that book, I will expand on the various narrative elements, give them my interpretation along with an additional dimension or twist, and include arguments from other sources.

Binary Opposition
According to anthropologist Claude Lévi-Strauss in his 1972 book *The Savage Mind*, the theory of human cognition

is based on binary opposites, in the sense that humans perceive reality by dividing everything into two mutually opposing groups.

Here are some examples: life-death, health-sickness, love-hate, freedom-slavery, wisdom-folly, truth-falsehood, courage-cowardice, treason-loyalty, and so on and so forth.

This binary opposition, which characterizes humankind's thought processes, governs the dualist principle at the core of stories; it is also the nucleus of every change that takes place in the various episodes of a story, and is one of the most important qualities of effective storytelling.

As early as the fourth century BC, Aristotle posited that drama cannot be sustained without change (or what he called peripeteia) – whether it is a transition from calamity to good fortune or from good fortune to calamity.

However, a change that creates a reversal of the values that are pivotal to a given episode – that reverses the charge of those values from positive to negative or vice versa – can constitute this fundamental component of a story.

In storytelling, we would do well to ensure that the change at the center of our story involves two opposing and mutually incompatible universal values. Thus, if the beginning of our story is anchored in a certain value, as the plot unfolds, this value must do an about-face and end up as its diametrical opposite, or to quote Aristotle himself, "the action veers round to its opposite."

Naturally, in the course of the story, it can flip back on itself several times, as often as every scene or episode. But as McKee stresses, it is this transition that makes a story interesting and worth telling.

And indeed, after examining a considerable amount of content, I was able to see clearly that pieces that incorporate the element of binary opposition are of superior quality.

If you try to recall stories that you have read, movies that you have watched, or even images that you have seen – the ones that you thought were good – and if you try to reconstruct and scrutinize their plots and isolate their factual frameworks, you will probably observe that they are based on binary opposition.

And since nothing illustrates an idea better than a story, here is an example of a clip in which binary opposition is as clear as sunlight on a bright morning. This item requires focus and concentration, because it contains almost no spoken language and possibly because it is not easy to digest. You are strongly encouraged to watch it before reading on.

"Most Shocking Second a Day Video" (Link 13)

So, what's happening here? Why is the element of binary opposition so vital? Why is it crucial to successful storytelling?

Possibly because it builds tension, prompts focus, and fosters concentration, but mainly because it renders the material easy to process and disambiguates interpretation – specifically due to its distinct duality.

Think about it. When you need to define a concept, the easiest way to do so is by stating its opposite. For instance: the opposite of small? Big! Precisely.

Moreover, for content consumers, the reversal of universal values at the center of a story gives rise to an illusion that in our lives, too, everything can suddenly turn around. That even if we haven't done so well for ourselves yet, there is still a possibility that we'll be transformed into superstars; if we are penniless, we can become rich; if we are ugly, we can become handsome; and so on. It is not surprising, then, that this is one of the most widely used elements in effective storytelling schemas. Thus, for example, it is central to the *Against all odds* category, specifically the *Cinderella* and *The underdog* schemas, as well as to the category of the Classic Story.

But what about the other way around? The transition from riches to poverty, from success to failure, from bliss to misery... What kind of illusion is provoked by this sort of reversal?

Such cases are more complex, in my opinion. If a character really deserves the negative reversal of fortune that befalls him, this is bound to induce an illusion that he had it coming, that there is justice in this world, that the righteous rejoice and the wicked perish, that righteous judgment is meted out by a higher power, and that in the end, order has been restored.

But what if the protagonist does not deserve a negative reversal, and her fate is unjust? What if everything seems unfair?

Such a scenario is likely to be perceived as a confirmation of what we already know: that life can be unfair and that bad things can happen not only to us but to others as well. This turn of events corroborates our understanding that our world is often unjust and thus, in many instances, spurs us to fight injustice, to rally against wrongdoing, to combat evil forces; in short, it prompts us to try to make the world a better place – as does the clip you have just watched about the girl whose world has been turned upside down.

It appears, then, that the binary opposition of this kind feeds into some fundamental psychological processes, some central aspects of human existence, irrespective of whether it follows a "happy ending" trajectory – as for example in the genre of the romantic novel – or culminates in bitterness and calamity.

If you need additional examples, there is no need to go far. In almost any successful story you can identify an opposing element, not only in the central plot but also in all the subplots – starting with the biblical tale of Adam and Eve's expulsion from the Garden of Eden and ending with the Brothers Grimm's fairy tales.

But why not find out for yourself?

Take any book, any movie, or any advertisement that you find fascinating, try to isolate its factual frame, and observe how binary opposition is conjured before your very eyes.

Order in Chaos

Bruner (2002) argues that, for humans, stories serve as an effective cognitive means for imagining scenarios that are likely to occur in reality. These situations include not only what is anticipated but also, and mainly, unexpected turns of events. They account for human behavior, both typical and idiosyncratic, present different options of dealing with it, and elucidate the common ground that makes it possible for people in a society, community, or culture to achieve mutual understanding.

In this way, stories "domesticate" the unexpected, thus cognitively enabling us to accommodate the strange or the bizarre, and also to a great extent to understand and to accept the unconventional and the unexpected.

As Nilli Diengott explains in "Narrative: an interdisciplinary perspective" (2010), following Bruner's line of thought, the tapestry of stories in a culture enables the existence of community life, inasmuch as stories make it possible to experience and accommodate all deviation and dissent in a controlled and safe manner.

Possibly, this rationale gave rise to McKee's assumption that a good story fulfills the human need to make sense out of life, to make order out of chaos, to provide a "recipe" for appropriate behavior.

As storytellers, we can learn from this principle, that when we tell a story, we must make sure that it includes a statement or a message that will offer an insight into life and shed light on our daily existence.

Universal Human Experience

One of the attributes of a story is its ability to transport us to a parallel universe that creates an illusion of reality, of another life that is parallel to ours yet can also represent ours. In other words, although a story includes specific characters, their feelings, thought processes, ambitions, and so on, in order to touch our audience, the story must be based on some kind of universal human experience.

Even if, at the outset, a character in our story is a stranger to the audience, as the story continues and that character develops, she must move closer to the audience. From being a foreigner, she must become more familiar; from being different than the audience, she must become akin to it – in actions, in apprehensions, and in thoughts, in all or some of her attributes and experiences.

Even if a character is diametrically different from the audience in all his characteristics and exploits, even if at first it might seem that the audience can feel nothing but disgust towards him – as his personality evolves with the unfolding of the plot, we can impel the audience to empathize with him or with the situations and feelings that he experiences.

Try to recall some movies or tales whose characters are so-called antiheroes – murderers, robbers, crooks – and for all that, you identified with them. Why did you? Maybe it is for the reason expressed in the quotation I mentioned earlier: that if a person hears someone else's story, they will feel an affinity with the latter in one way or another. And also maybe because villains, too, can manifest the human anguish that we all have experienced at some point in our lives, because, when all is said and done, a human being remains a human being.

In sum, a story constitutes a microcosm in which we find all the elements of our own lives. Through a story, we exist for a short while in a parallel universe that gives license to or even endorses our beliefs, behaviors, and the like – and without exacting the price we would pay if we ventured to attain the same experiences in real life. Or, as McKee puts it, stories "fulfill a profound human need to grasp the patterns of living – not merely as an intellectual exercise, but within a very personal, emotional experience."

An Event Brought About by or Affecting a Character

In light of the above discussion, and in line with Labov's generic mapping of the story, every story must include some pivotal event, a change, or a complication. This point should by now be very clear. Yet it appears that, for McKee at least, this is not enough. In his approach, in order for such an event or twist to make a real difference, it must either be precipitated by or affect a character in the story, otherwise the effect will be lost.

Why so?

To evoke empathy.

Because the truth is that stories in which something important happens to an inanimate object rarely, if ever, touch our hearts.

For example, take a flood. Let's imagine that somewhere on earth it rained as long and as hard as in the biblical story of Noah's Ark, but no towns were harmed. If that were the scenario in the Bible, the lives of animals and humans would not have been endangered, and Noah wouldn't have had to build his ark in the first place. What's all the fuss about, then? So there was a flood. It still would have caused some destruction, but wouldn't warrant a special mention, as is the case when living things are hurt.

In my view, the only types of content that can captivate us without containing events that are caused by or affect a character are the ones that provide an aesthetic experience, which serves as a substitute of a sort. Such content can serve as a vehicle for conveying a desired meaning only in specific circumstances, mainly on visual platforms; moreover, in order to be effective, it needs to include entities endowed with awareness, a background context, and associative visual-aesthetic elements.

However, there is more to the rationale that the pivotal event or change needs either to be triggered by or influence a character. Such a scenario also enables us to map the character's personality; it promotes further action and thus elicits a response from both other characters and the audience, evoking feelings. In other words, it serves as an impetus that drives the story forward.

Ultimately, what helps us understand a character the best is not what she says about herself or what the narrator tells about her, but how she acts, and mainly in response to the stress resulting from the pivotal event or change. Such circumstances reveal a character's true personality, and this is also where the content creator can carve out a distinctive and compelling image for our character, one that our audiences will find worthwhile to hear about and follow.

Let me demonstrate this through a story, in this case not a movie. Below is a short passage that I wrote in such a way as to conjure the protagonist's image from the narrative fabric of the text. This kind of exercise is possible when the character is vivid or when their escapades are perceived as dramatic because they involve some social or cultural deviation.

My mother was an extravagant person. Different, unconventional. And that's how she lived.

Once, when I was a child, she took me with her on a shopping trip to the big city. I remember entering a luxury fashion boutique that sold imported clothes, the sight of which took my breath away. I stood there staring at the glamorous garments on display and felt like Alice in Wonderland.

But what about my mother?

She nonchalantly handled the fabric of several dresses, and taking down a tight-fitting gown whose skirt, starting at the knee, swelled out in flowing waves and flounces of fancy muslin, looked it over with a critical eye. The saleslady rushed to her side, and after making sure that my mother was aware of the item's steep price, started extolling its unique cut, rare texture, detailed workmanship, and the intellectual depth of the French designer who created this paragon of perfection.

And what about my mother?

She cocked her head to one side as if in deliberation, then entered the fitting room, donned the dress, came out, and positioned herself in front of the mirror. She looked at herself in profile, first right, then left, turned around, and then stood still. All the while, the saleslady praised the dress in superlative terms.

Then my mother leaned forward, grabbed the hem of the glamourous gown with her two robust hands, and in a single sharp movement ripped off the muslin trimming attached to it. Then – as we watched agape – she straightened up and pronounced: "Now it is really perfect." Whereupon, with serene equanimity, she walked over to the cash register, took out her wallet, looked the saleslady in the eye, and asked: "What did you say the price was?"

Why did I tell you this particular story?

Compare the opening sentences – "My mother was an extravagant person. Different, unconventional. And so was everything she did" – with the narration of the character in action. The heroine's conduct speaks for itself, and her image rises out of the textual detail. It seems, then, that this story does not require a preamble about the heroine; without these, it is equally compelling, powerful, and persuasive. But would it work the other way around? Not so much.

When an event is provoked by or has an impact upon a character, it not only provides us, as narrators, with the opportunity to animate that character, flesh her out, and make her actions speak for themselves; it also elicits a more intense engagement and a stronger sense of identification in the audience.

And this brings us to the next narrative quality: identification.

Identification

One of the essential elements in effective storytelling is the ability to involve the audience in the story emotionally, and the most straightforward way to achieve this is by making them identify with the characters. If we are unable to create an affinity between the audience and our story's characters, it will be difficult to evoke their emotions. An audience will become emotionally involved in the events portrayed in a story only if they identify with its protagonist and other heroes.

According to McKee, the audience identifies with the protagonist not out of pity or compassion, not on account of his trials and tribulations, as set out in Aristotle's algorithm, but because in that character we see ourselves, our own reflection. In other words, the audience's emotional engagement with the story is motivated not by altruism or sympathy, but by personal reasons and possibly even egocentrism.

McKee argues that, when the audience identifies with the hero and his desires, they in effect celebrate their own desires, and this identification enables them to project themselves into a fictional entity, thereby both probing and extending their own humanity.

Some readers will justifiably conclude that this effect ultimately brings about the Aristotelian catharsis, the longed-for release of tension.

The Main Point of the Story

For those who are hesitant to accept my extended definition of the coda, the main point of the story is presented here as a separate element.

According to Bruner (2002), this is essentially the addressees' retrospective evaluation of the story's import, and it can be either implicit or stated overtly. Either way, every story must have a punchline, and all roads in the story must eventually lead to it.

The question to ask yourself is, "What makes your story worth telling?"

What will the reader gain by reading your story?

In a punchline, we can infuse our truth – our values, our credo, our distinctive outlook on life, our message.

Here is an example of such a punchline in a post from my personal blog:

> Yesterday, I had a corrective experience. Inversely corrective, that is.
>
> What do I mean by that?
>
> Until yesterday, the distribution of responsibilities in our household was clear. Some of the work was done by my husband, and some by me. Each of us had a preset role, and each task was clearly marked and labeled. One of the chores that was the exclusive purview of my spouse, at least until yesterday, was to scale and clean fish. A dubious pleasure, as most people will agree. A typically male job, if you ask me. If it were up to me, these vermin would never be allowed past my doorstep unless they had first been thoroughly disinfected, scrubbed, and fumigated. Accordingly, everyone in the household has always clearly understood that whoever wishes to consume fish has to fulfil this odoriferous obligation.
>
> But then... something happened yesterday.

Actually, it had started two days earlier with a complaint from my husband about a stuffed nose, but culminated yesterday in complete disability. It doesn't really matter what they are sick with; as soon as they catch even the slightest illness, they turn into a useless sack of potatoes. Oh well, what else can you expect of men?

But – the fish that had arrived at our doorstep yesterday morning re-materialized on the kitchen counter before my bewildered eyes. When I finally regained my powers of understanding, I shoved the whole package deep in the bottom shelf of the fridge. A desolate spot. As far as I was concerned, it could stay there forevermore, like a stone in the wilderness. However, with the approach of suppertime, a nagging thought infiltrated my consciousness: "If my daughters' IQ is my top priority, I must fulfill the sacred obligation and clean that fish. After all," I said to myself naively, "cleaning a few fish is a minor sacrifice for enriching my daughters' grey matter with omega-3 oils!"

I am a good, even exemplary, mother, aren't I?! Would I deprive my offspring of the salubrious benefit of vital nutrients?! No! A thousand times no! I squared my shoulders and martyred myself in the name of my offspring's well-being.

I was hoping that, by the time my daughters got back from the theater, I would be ready for them with a nourishing meal. Wallowing in self-pity, yet undaunted and full of determination, I rolled up my sleeves and set out to clean the fish.

What is there left to say?

Only that all the fish should go back to the sea where they came from and that omega-3 should be consumed in the form of castor oil or cod liver oil or free-range eggs or any damned nutritional supplement conjured by scientists.

That day I learned that cleaning fish is hard physical work, revolting and malodorous. Scales flew in every direction and, like cruise missiles, hit me on the head, the face, the eyelids; they got into my nostrils, stuck fast in my hair, and clung for life to my clothes. For hours afterwards, my hands stank of fish, and two days later the smell still lingered inside my nostrils.

At the end of my labors, the kitchen looked like a battlefield, and what about me? I looked and felt like a soldier suffering from battle shock. Smudges of blood covered the kitchen counter, and fish flesh was everywhere: in the sink, on the utensils, on the floor. It took me some time to realize that the blood was actually mine, from a cut. I wrapped a bandage around my throbbing hand (all the while trying to shun gloomy thoughts of blood poisoning and amputated fingers), fried the fish, and prepared mashed potatoes and a wholesome, finely chopped salad.

Just as I had finished, the door flew open, and like a whirlwind into the kitchen charged my babies, happy and sprightly, carrying in their outstretched hands – an enormous box containing a family-size pizza.

Now that the point of the story is clear, read it again and observe how its every aspect leads to the climactic ending.

This punchline I associate with McKee's idea that, when a story has run its course, it must offer us an insight about ourselves, our existence, our life. Essentially, it is this universal statement, the message that the story carries over, that renders it relevant not only for us but for many other individuals as well.

That's all as far as narrative qualities are concerned.

You are probably rubbing your hands together again, eager to jump on the wagon. However, I am compelled to stop you. Again. So sorry! True, you and I have already covered a considerable distance: we have learned that storytelling pays off, that telling stories is easier when using schemas, and that any story we tell must be cognitively "nourishing," in the sense that it needs to contain staple elements. But what about seasoning? The crucial importance of seasoning cannot be overstressed.

Why?

Not only because a bland story is unpalatable, but because it is seasoning that ensures that a story is good, even if it is not built according to the schemas for effective storytelling.

"What is she talking about?" you are probably wondering. "Is she out of her mind?" After all this, am I now saying that storytelling can be effective even without using the schemas?

But of course!

Good storytelling is not subject to a narrow and restrictive set of inflexible rules; there is only a general direction, some guidelines. Same as in life. One can decide to adhere to the rules of a good, healthy, and happy life; but does this mean that one cannot live a good, healthy, and happy life without following such rules?

As I mentioned in the previous chapter, the ingredients that we have added to the pot so far are not enough. In order for the food to be tasty, it needs to be spiced up with what I term here "narrative seasoning."

What are these spices without which a story will miss its mark even though it has all the other necessary ingredients?

12

Narrative Seasoning

Before I discuss these "narrative spices," I would like to throw at you one of the questions I almost invariably get in my lectures and workshops on strategic storytelling and which has probably been troubling you as well, buzzing somewhere at the back of your mind.

Where do you find stories, for Pete's sake?

Well, you're right, it's a million-dollar question.

Even if you deeply internalize the guidelines for effective storytelling that I have presented here, if you follow Labov's roadmap, if you incorporate all the elements discussed by McKee and implement Aristotle's directives, even if you master the use of the seasoning that I am about to describe –

Where the hell do stories come from?

Unlike babies, stories are not delivered by storks.

But you don't need to lounge around waiting for inspiration. I will also not implore you to think out of the box, to use your imagination, or to be creative, though if you are capable of any of these feats – great! They can come in handy. Instead, I will tell you what I usually tell anyone who asks me this question:

Don't invent; find!

Think of your life as an arsenal of stories, and you will realize that the trick is not to invent stories but to choose points from your life that are worth telling about.

Let me explain – through a story, of course.

In one lecture that I gave to a group of managers, someone I knew was in the audience. In the beginning, he seemed rather pleased that he and the lecturer were on friendly terms. However, when I told my audience that stories were not to be invented but rather found, I noticed that he made a skeptical face.

After the lecture, I came up to him and asked about the reason for his apparent incredulity. He looked down his nose at me and said: "What do you take me for, Osnat? Telling us to find and not to invent! In your life, something is always happening – everyone knows that. Do you think that we are all like that?"

I looked him straight in the eye and retorted without a moment's hesitation...

That he was right. That my life is really like a movie, and I would beat the bejeezus out of the director if I should ever manage to lay my hands on him!

"But the truth is," I went on – and quoted the famous American radio broadcaster Ira Glass, "Great stories happen to those who can tell them."

Why am I telling you all that?

Because the most appealing spice in our stories is precisely that we find rather than invent them. It is a seasoning that includes a little bit of everything. If you have this seasoning, you won't need to add anything else, except maybe salt.

Authenticity

Authenticity is effortless if your story is not a replica, because it is an original product. Moreover, authenticity is expressed not only in what you have to say but in the way you say it.

Simply put, do not copy others. If you can find stories in what has happened in your life, in your experiences, in occurrences that you were involved in, witnessed, or heard about, your stories are bound to be authentic. Because, when all is said and done, these are your stories – no one can tell them the same way as you. You are the one and only. And along the way, you obtain another ingredient, credibility.

Credibility

When you recount an episode you witnessed, an incident that happened to you or your client, you will present it credibly because your narrative is based on personal experience. Even if you were a bystander at an event involving a different protagonist, you are relaying it firsthand. In such a case, to tell the story credibly and effectively there is no need to invent sensations or feelings, or to put yourself in the protagonist's place and try to imagine what she must have felt.

Integrity

Integrity is the third side of the triangle that, together with authenticity and credibility, constitutes the seasoning we spoke about earlier. It is a subjective dimension in the aspect of storytelling discussed in this chapter.

We could find an excellent story, both authentic and credible – but does our integrity allow us to divulge it to the public? In other words, you need to ask yourself whether you believe this story. Are you at liberty to tell it? Does this story represent your credo, your values? If the answers to all these questions are affirmative, you are heading in the right direction. Because telling stories that we have no business telling hurts our credibility; and if we are at liberty to tell them but they don't reflect our values or credo – what's the point of telling them in the first place?

Remember: Being a good storyteller is great but not

enough; we also need to know how to choose the right story, one that will further our goals.

Yet, the equilateral triangle with authenticity, credibility, and integrity as its sides cannot be left without a core, a beating heart at its center; and this is vulnerability.

Vulnerability

Vulnerability is about our ability and willingness to show others our human weakness. One could object that, by exposing our weak points, we put ourselves on the spot, because we acknowledge our fears, apprehensions, failures, dreams, and aspirations. It is as if we were opening ourselves up to criticism, ridicule, and scorn. However, what we are actually doing is placing a mirror before our audience, one that reflects their own fears, confusion, and uncertainty, and possibly also their lack of courage to acknowledge that they are made of exactly the same stuff as we are.

Open Facebook and take a look at your feed. If you disregard all your friends' reposts, all the commercials and advertisements, and focus only on what your friends are willing to share about themselves, you will find that it is mainly their successes – overseas trips, festive occasions, business gains, talented children, a happy life. Now tell me frankly, hand on heart: Is that what makes you identify with these people? Do these posts make you want to run and give them a big and loving hug? Maybe – if they are very close to you. But what about the rest? What about the others, who – let's face it – probably make up the majority of your Facebook friends?

When you tell a story on Facebook, you are not targeting only the narrow circle of your close friends and associates, right? Because these people are already a captive audience.

You should keep in mind, then, that the vulnerability we reveal in our stories invests them with tremendous power. Paradoxically, the weaknesses that we allow others to see give our story, and therefore also ourselves, the power to touch others. Because by showing that we are vulnerable, we also admit that we are human and thus convey to our audience: Look at me and you will see yourself.

I cannot stress enough how important it is to share your own stories with others! This is what will enable you to be authentic and credible, to get in touch with your own feelings, to show that you are vulnerable, and thereby also to reach your audience. Besides, if you tell your own stories, no one can say, "I have already heard this a thousand times."

So are we ready now? Do we have all the chapters of the manual for effective storytelling under our belts?

The answer, for a change, is yes.

That is, of course, if your objective is not to promote an agenda or advance a goal by means of a story.

If you do have such a purpose – and this is precisely what this book is about – it would be wise to continue reading. In the next chapter, I present tools for strategic storytelling with a view of promoting agendas and goals – in life, at work, and in business.

Because, in the end, we must add salt to our dish, right?

O. G. GOAZ

13

Promoting Agendas and Goals

You may have heard of the Sapir-Whorf hypothesis, which states that the structure of the language we use influences our modes of thought and outlook. In other words, language determines our cognitive processes and the way we see the world.

Alternatively, you may believe that language is but an expression of thought, that it reinforces existing perceptions and entrenches the status quo.

Although these two theories lie on opposite sides of a theoretical and ideological spectrum, they both conceive of language, both spoken and written, as a powerful force. The trick is to learn how to harness this power to promote one's agendas and goals.

The first condition for achieving this successfully is awareness.

At issue is an awareness of our decisions – starting with a conscious choice about which story to tell and including the way of telling it, what to include and what to omit, and finally the lexicon, the phraseology, and the examples we will be using.

Let's put it this way: The basic guideline for furthering agendas and goals is to remember that the choice of a specific phrase or expression must always have a motivation behind it. Invariably, there are a number of ways to say the same thing, and your choice of words must never be arbitrary. Every time we say something, our decision on how to do so must be valid in terms of reason as well as purpose. There must be intention and direction behind everything we say, even if it might appear otherwise to our listeners.

And yes, such an approach requires an investment of thought and effort; it compels us to express ourselves – in terms of phraseology, style, structure, and so on – with great precision. Yet to the extent that we want to lead our audience to a desired goal, this is what we must do.

This undertaking might appear less daunting if I tell you that, at least in my experience, although such mental scrutiny might at first take a lot of time, with practice it will become much easier. As is the case with many other things in life, making conscious and deliberate linguistic choices will eventually become second nature to you.

Now, let's assume that we have made all of our choices with due awareness – can we be assured that our audience will accept what we say in the way we intended it?

In truth, in spite of our efforts to guide our audience to support our agenda, it is important to realize that a story inherently lends itself to different perceptions and interpretations. This is because a story cannot serve as a vehicle for a single, fixed meaning, insofar as its interpretation largely depends on the listener's characteristics and skills.

To put it differently, the processing of a story requires the addressee to interpret it using the means at their disposal and in light of their values, perceptions, and familiarity with the sociocultural context in which that story is recounted. This means that different addressees will process the same story differently. But even so, the narrator – us, in this case – has the wherewithal to reduce the set of feasible meanings and guide our target audience towards an intended interpretation.

As content creators, we cannot ensure that the audience will interpret our stories as intended, but we operate on the premise advanced by Stuart Hall in his 1982 essay "The Rediscovery of 'Ideology': Return of the Repressed in Media Studies" that it is possible to induce a preferred meaning. That is, our storytelling choices can minimize the scope of meanings that otherwise could be unlimited. As Umberto Eco put it in his 1992 book *Interpretation and Overinterpretation*, we can lead the audience to concur with the meaning that the text endorses or, at the very least, to agree upon the meanings that are not supported.

Now let us see how we can apply our knowledge in practice. What means are there to make our story guide the addressees along the path we want them to follow to a destination of our choice? This is accomplished by using what Bruner (1991) terms "narrative baiting." At issue here is the arrangement and organization of the discourse, the use of algorithms and dramatic tools, the ways of charging the text with emotion, and strategies that will impel the audience to "follow" the narrator.

In order to understand what is involved in narrative baiting, we must familiarize ourselves with the various levels of awareness that we, as content creators, need to achieve.

Awareness of Narrative Choices

Know why you are telling what you are telling.

We must be aware of the purpose of everything we are relaying. Our aims can be numerous and varied, such as propelling the plot forward, creating tension, gaining attention, eliciting engagement, and elucidating or explaining the various elements of our story.

This awareness must be at the narrative level – that is, we need to know why we are telling what we are telling and be able to answer the following questions: What purpose is served by each part of the content that we have created? What is it designed to achieve or promote in the story? Is it meant to arouse the addressees' curiosity? To provide an explanation? To inform them? And so on.

Awareness of Semiotic Choices

Get to know your audience.

We need to be aware which content resonates with extra-textual symbolic and semiotic frameworks, in order to ensure that our audience will understand our story in the cultural-social-environmental context in which it is told. We absolutely must know who our target audience is, otherwise we might be sabotaging not only our own attempts to direct them along an intended decoding trajectory but also their understanding of the story itself. This is because storytelling requires that the addressees be familiar with the extra-narrative symbolic and semiotic frameworks within which the story is told.

Imagine, for example, that I tell a group of people who have no knowledge whatsoever about Israel or Israelis a story incorporating elements that demand some familiarity with Israeli culture, such as common military jargon used in the Israeli army. How well do you think they will be able to interpret the messages I want to convey through my story if they lack the wherewithal to decode them?

Awareness of Rhetorical Choices

Choose rhetorical means appropriate to your agenda.

This kind of choice requires an awareness that no two words are the same. Imagine a set of scales: on one side, place the term "household help" and on the other "handmaid." Will the scale stay balanced, in your opinion? Is the word "handmaid" equivalent to "household help"? Or is it possible that the word "handmaid" has connotations that charge it with meanings that are absent from the other expression?

This example shows that some words have positive connotations and others negative, and that therefore words can be vehicles for positive and negative effects. Clearly, we need to be aware of the charge that some words may carry and the power that other words can wield, and make informed and conscious use of this potential to get our message across and promote our agenda.

This aspect will be discussed in detail below, but I want to point out here that a writer has at her disposal a wide range of tools to inject words with feeling and to select phraseology that is loaded with connotations, evokes associations, and arouses emotions.

In order to guide our addressees to the destination that we want them to reach, we must make informed use of narrative baiting to ensure that the mental picture of the story that is formed in their minds accords with our design. To perform this task successfully, we must make conscious choices regarding the structure, phraseology, and lexicon of our discourse and anchor our story's content in a context familiar to our audience. In this way, we can render our story perceptible to the mind's eye of our addressees, much like a storyboard used in planning advertising. This is important, because humans tend believe what they see.

To this end, it is essential to master the techniques for creating a mental picture, one that can prompt the reader to accept the writer's stance, approach, and point of view. Such strategies encompass various linguistic-rhetorical elements, as well as links to symbols, myths, cultural and social codes, and intertextual contexts.

Within the story that we are telling, these means can be conceptualized on two levels: overt and covert.

Layers in Storytelling

The overt layer of a story
This is the level of our story's structural foundation – the facts, the data, the events. Here, the story takes shape as a function of the linguistic and narrative content through which it is expressed. In other words, it is the level at which the text is processed literally, without interpreting its deeper meaning. It is the level at which the story is recounted, its independent variable, which scholars of narrative call the "diegetic level."

The covert layer of a story
This level of a story contains encrypted messages that the narrator seeks to convey through the content and that encapsulate the story's agenda, aim, objectives, and ideology. This is also the level at which the story influences the addressees and impels them to take a side – by marking the persecutor and the persecuted, the truth and the falsehood, the right and the wrong. This is essentially the dependent variable of the story, the level at which we get messages across, generate contexts, and lead our audience to an intended destination.

The Means

I divide the rhetorical means that are available to us as storytellers to achieve a desired effect into four main categories:

- *Cognitive tools:* persuasion using facts and data, which in Aristotle's theory is the logos;
- *Emotive tools:* projecting and evoking feeling through the use of tropes, dramatic elements, and so on, an element in Aristotle's framework termed pathos;
- *Structural-stylistic tools:* the choice of genre, style, and structure; the arranging and ordering of the story's text to serve a pre-set purpose.

- *Illustration:* I distinguish three kinds of such tools – verbal exemplification, visual illustration, and elucidation using voice and body language. These three means serve to reinforce the others (cognitive, emotive, and structural-stylistic), and at the same time to validate the ethos, which is the third and last dimension in Aristotle's theory of rhetoric.

Before describing the above tools in detail, an explanation of Aristotle's theory is in order. We need to become familiar with this framework because all theories of persuasion ultimately derive from it.

Theoretical investigations of persuasion tend to emphasize logos and pathos as the two primary dimensions of Aristotle's system, and ethos as supplementary. My analysis is slightly different and is aligned with Megan McIntyre and Jessica McKee's approach, presented in their article entitled "Ethos: Appeals to Authority and Credibility": I employ two subcategories of ethos – authority and credibility – and attach each to a different rhetorical tool.

I align logos – persuasion through an appeal to reason – with the concept of "telling" widely used in literary research, or the sense of authority.

Pathos – enticement through an appeal to feelings – can be conceptualized as "showing," or the sense of credibility.

Telling

The definition of "telling" is just as you'd assume it to be: the act of relaying events and facts, presenting proof, and displaying data.

In telling a story, the narrator does not employ dramatic means. Rather than presenting events and dialogue directly, the narrator moderates the information by relaying an episode and then summarizing the narration. This element is rather dry, akin to reporting facts in the order in which they occurred in reality.

In my approach, to employ this element effectively to persuade our audience and lead them where we wish them to be, the narrator often needs to be an expert or an authority figure – or to be perceived as such. This, in a nutshell, is my first subcategory of ethos, in the sense of the narrator's authority in the subject matter discussed.

Showing

In the context of storytelling, "showing" means engaging a wide range of senses and sensibilities to induce in the audience the experience of reality. Through the use of rhetorical tools, the present tense, and direct quotes, as well as by representing episodes in a manner that allows visualization and by illustrating feelings and ambience, the narrator can create an illusory effect of truth, bringing the audience closer to the narrative.

When showing, the narrator presents events directly and lets the audience draw their own conclusions from what they hear and see, without moderating the process. In storytelling, this element has the power to create the illusion of truth. One could think of it as "translating" what is going on in reality into spoken language. The ethos salient in this context is in the sense of credibility perceived vis-à-vis the narrator or the narration.

Here is an example.

Using telling, a narrator could say "Jane was afraid"; showing, on the other hand, would appear something like this: "Jane's heart was about to burst out of her chest, her forehead was covered in a cold sweat, and her hands shook uncontrollably."

As you can observe, the portrayal of Jane's fear in the second variant is more vivid and dramatic than in the first; it gives rise to a visual image and urges the addressees to infer independently that Jane was afraid.

Instead of informing the audience that 2+2=4, the narrator leads them to reach this conclusion by themselves. In this way, the addressees become engaged in the story and, to some extent, come to "own" it.

In showing, the narrator's role is downplayed, to the point that they are not perceived as taking part in storytelling at all; instead, the story appears to be telling itself, and in some parts even to be told by the audience.

The act of showing can be compared to a camera that documents and thus immortalizes every moment of an episode being filmed.

And here lies an advantage of showing over telling as a rhetorical tool: showing enables the narrator to attain a degree of credibility, reality, and truth. This does not mean that we as narrators, or what we are telling, are actually credible or true.

Logos demands a sense of the narrator's authority, professionalism, and credentials (either real or perceived), which can take a long time to achieve; it is a dimension that is located outside the story and is a function of who we are or how we are seen by others, or of the way we wear our authority on our sleeve in our encounter with the audience.

Pathos, on the other hand, calls for a sense of credibility in the narrator and the narration, and it is a function of our ability to create the illusion of truth through the content we create within the story – in the intra-textual dimension – by using narrative and the rhetorical tools at our disposal.

It should be clear, then, that even if you possess the first subcategory of ethos, authority, you might find it difficult to promote your agenda, unless you are also capable of attaining the other kind of ethos, credibility.

At the same time, if you have credibility, you will be able to promote your agenda even without authority.

Think for a moment. How often have you sat in front of an accredited professional – one of those people with a penchant for displaying a framed diploma for everyone to see, such as a lawyer – without believing a word he was saying?

And conversely, how is it conceivable that rapists, murderers, and thieves manage, time after time, to sell their agenda by professing innocence – for example, through the media – even though their authority is for all intents and purposes nonexistent?

So, in your opinion, which of the two kinds of ethos is easier to come by?

We focus on the use of elements that enable us to promote our agenda and goals through enticement – that is, pathos – so that their effect operates under the radar, circumventing rational reasoning and thus dodging objections on the part of the audience.

In essence, rhetoric is a way to achieve credibility without taking the trouble to obtain the requisite authority. This is not to say that having authority is a bad thing; authority can be very, very helpful, but it is important to remember that it is not authority that is likely to win you the audience's trust.

In light of the above discussion, what strategic storytelling means do we have at our disposal?

Cognitive tools

These include all the data, proof, research, facts. In my workshops and lectures on storytelling as a strategic tool, I term them "rational anchors," and in that connection mention Robert M. Pirsig's novel *Zen and the Art of Motorcycle Maintenance: An Inquiry into Values*. The author presents a rational and a romantic approach side by side and analyzes the phenomenon of sunset by its component parts and factors. Such cognitive means rely on content comprising quantitative data, facts, proof – elements that include dates, numbers, time periods, locations, technical information, and so forth.

This tool does not require further explanation. In my experience, and probably also in yours, most posters, presentations, and lectures follow this pattern: dry facts and data marked by bullets. PowerPoint presentations are structured in exactly the same way – bullet points.

Emotive tools

Appeal to affect works like magic, in the sense that the message is usually accepted by the audience without any effort on the part of the narrator. I like to draw an analogy with injecting a substance directly into the brain or, if you prefer, into the heart. The literature enumerates dozens of tools that belong to this group, but here I will introduce only the most widespread, subdividing them into two sets: (a) figurative language, or tropes – verbal images – and (b) linguistic choices, context, and intertextual elements.

a) Figurative language or tropes – verbal images

These are rhetorical tools we use for elucidating through description or for illustrating a subject, a concept, or a feeling that is recondite, complex, or difficult to grasp. Tropes are among the most effective ways to reach people's hearts, to establish a connection, and to elicit engagement – because their power lies in creating a verbal image in the minds of the addressees.

People mostly believe what they see – remember?

Below are several common ways to achieve a desired effect:

- *Imagery:* metaphors, similes, and analogies. These tools have served interpersonal communication from time immemorial and are widely available and universally accessible. Imagery can be effective in illustrating concepts that are abstract, do not lend themselves to simple explanation, or need to be discussed in detail to be understood.

This rhetorical means plays an important role in human thought and cognitive processes related to comprehension. In addition to its expressive functions, imagery has the power to scale down information and evoke visual mental pictures.

Let me give you an example. Once, when my youngest daughter was in preparatory school, I got an email from the teacher saying that "Amelia the louse has come for a visit" and that all parents were requested to take measures. Promptly, I whisked my daughter into the shower, washed her hair, and subjected her scalp to a rigorous examination using a lice comb to search for incriminating evidence. This I found. Quite a bit of it. All those lice caught in the teeth of the comb gave me a real shock, and I spontaneously commented in singsong, "A jungle has sprouted on your head!"

Precisely a year after this happened, we got another email from the same teacher phrased in exactly the same way. I did everything I had done a year before but, to my great relief, didn't find any signs of infestation and jubilantly announced to my daughter that her head was lice-free. She sighed contentedly and said, "That's lucky, mom! Last time you told me that I had a jungle on my head – and I couldn't sleep all night."

The image of a head sprouting a jungle was so powerful that not only was the child unable to sleep at night but she remembered my exact words a year later. That's how compelling imagery can be. So when you tell stories, keep in mind that imagery has enormous power: it renders abstract and complex expressions or notions concrete; it distills information; it juxtaposes one conceptual universe with another. This is what we call a rhetorical means – a tool that can translate reality for us, create its visual representation, and thereby affect our subconscious. This is what invests our discourse with forcefulness that exceeds the power wielded by lexical meanings alone.

What, then, is the difference among the various kinds of imagery?

Analogies and similes create complex verbal pictures of two entities or contexts from altogether different spheres and compare them to each other, with a view to emphasizing their similarities and/or differences. Similes usually include the word "like" or "as" or an equivalent phrase. For example: "She abandoned me as if I were a dog" or "like a lion in a cage." Metaphor, on the other hand, involves transferring a subject (also termed "tenor," "ground," or "target," depending on the discipline) to the semantic field of anther subject ("vehicle," "figure," or "source"), without the use of a phrase signaling comparison. It functions as a condensed verbal picture merging the meanings of two completely different entities, for example, "hands of gold," "a wooden face," "the wheels of justice."

- *Encoding symbols:* These elements are part of a semiotic framework shaped by the conventions of a culture or a society and can be used to promote a desired interpretation. In other words, by encoding symbols within a story, we can lead the audience to produce ideological interpretations within the range acceptable to us.

In his essay "Rhetoric of the Image" (1977), Barthes discusses the use of these elements in advertising. As an example, he shows how pasta manufacturer Panzani in France devises ads replete with encoded symbols and myths to promote their products. One of the images incorporates the colors of the Italian flag – green, white, and red – to establish a subconscious link in the minds of consumers and thereby create the feeling that the pasta comes from Italy, even though in fact it is produced in France.

- *Personification:* This term describes a representation of animals, plants, or inanimate objects as humans or assigning them human characteristics. Personification impels us to identify and empathize with the entities or objects in question, both material and virtual. The power one can attain by using this trope is demonstrated in the following clip:

"If Google Was a Guy" (Link 14)

In this clip, Google is presented as a man who is expected to provide an answer to each query addressed to the eponymous internet tool. The clip is amusing and embarrassing all at once, and the representation of the Google search engine as a person oddly makes us identify with and feel empathy towards an algorithm.

- *Hyperbole:* A verbal picture can also be generated through the use of hyperbole, or exaggeration, a tool that helps leave a lasting imprint on an addressee's consciousness and shift the focus to where we want it to be directed. For example, "I've been waiting for hours," "I've asked you to do it a million times." Hyperbole can also take the form of exaggerated descriptions or unnecessary explanations.

- *Sarcasm or ridicule*: Sometimes hyperbole engenders sarcasm or ridicule, strategies that must be used with caution. In many instances, for example, on Facebook, I have seen sarcasm miss its mark; this happens for the most part when it is used in relation to politics or ideology, but not just in those contexts. Only last weekend, I was involved in an episode in which sarcasm was not recognized for what it was. The individual who committed this blunder happens to be a close relative of mine.

In the course of a leisurely chat, the person in question told some friends how he had once prompted me to do a flexibility exercise and how afterwards, my back was out for a fortnight – whereupon I corrected him with a serious mien,

"Not for a fortnight; for a year." I used linguistic exaggeration to generate sarcasm in retaliation for the hyperbole the speaker himself had used.

However, my mocking tone completely missed its mark, as became obvious from his subsequent remark addressed to our friends: "Did you hear that? A year. For a whole year she hobbled around with a sore back. So you be careful when doing this exercise." At that point, I was rolling on the floor laughing hysterically, and it took me at least ten minutes to calm down completely.

- *Rhyme and play on speech sounds:* It might come as a surprise, but this rhetorical tool has been shown to have a substantial impact on audiences. A study on rhyming demonstrated that audiences tend to accept information in the form of rhymes as more correct and credible – as the truth!

Surprising, isn't it?

Logically, this might be hard to understand, but if we think about it more seriously, we will realize that, when words and sentences rhyme, they are absorbed much more easily and deeply.

- *Oxymoron:* This rhetorical device conjoins opposite or contradictory concepts or phrases to create a new expression that is essentially paradoxical. Such a technique introduces a surprise element and usually leaves a strong impression on the addressees. Among the better known examples are "a thunderous silence," "a short wait," "a happy divorce," "sweet agony," "alone together," and more.

Needless to say, there are countless other tropes that can be used, but in my experience, the ones I listed here are highly effective and are easily implemented. They are also very common in advertising – which attests to their forcefulness.

b) Linguistic choices, intertextuality, symbols, and myths
Our decisions regarding the use of language in storytelling play an important role in shaping public opinion. These include linguistic choices: Which terms shall we use to describe a given situation or recount a particular episode? And here we are talking not only about lexical choices, such as "disengagement" instead of "withdrawal," or "demonstrators" as opposed to "inciters," but also semantic maneuvering, for example, the use of ambiguous words, which are common in marketing discourse, or preference for emotively charged terms.

The use of ambiguous language for rhetorical purposes is common in advertising. However, for this device to be effective, one must keep in mind that decoding it is contingent on the addressee's familiarity with the subject matter discussed and the context involved.

- *Connotation:* The term "connotation" is normally used to refer to the socio-cultural meaning of a word or a concept. It is an associated or secondary meaning that is usually shared by a group of speakers and is specific to time, culture, historical period, and other related parameters. Thus, for anyone over forty, the phrase "woman of the street" clearly alludes to the world's oldest profession, while today's seventeen-year-olds might not even know what we are talking about. Similarly, the synonymous but dated term "strumpet" may be more easily understood by an older person or by one who reads novels written several centuries ago.

- *Communication competence:* This aspect requires that we take into account the cultural and historical associations a term evokes in an addressee's mind. Knowing the literal, dictionary meaning of a word (denotation) is clearly not enough: it is important to anticipate the associative responses it may evoke.

How can we use all these possibilities to our advantage? It's actually rather simple. We can use words rich in connotations in order to arouse feelings or create cognitive shortcuts in the minds of our audience. Thus, for example, if I tell you a story about two friends and call them Cain and Abel, it is quite clear that I am exploiting the connotations of these names and intend to evoke associations attached to the biblical characters. And all this can be achieved without a single word of explanation.

By naming the characters, I have effectively marked them as bad and good, respectively. Note, however, that in doing so I have made no definite commitment, and am at liberty to reverse the roles later on in the plot, thus flouting the conventional associative patterns and creating a surprise effect. Yet, capitalizing on the connotative meaning of these names clearly affords me, as a narrator, a shortcut to fostering expectations, shaping perceptions, and achieving better communication with my audience.

- *Synonyms:* This term usually describes words with similar meaning, according to the premise that an entity can be designated by several signifiers. Normally, synonyms are analyzed as differing along several semantic axes.

Denotive – in the sense that each synonym signifies a slightly different concept, for example, "to look" vs. "to observe," or "intelligible" vs. "comprehensible."

Register – words with identical denotation that differ in terms of style and tone, such as the vernacular compared to the formal, as in "buy" vs. "purchase," or "quick" vs. "speedy."

Emotive – words that are denotively the same but differ in emotive connotation, for example, "house" vs. "home," "assistant" vs. "lackey."

Below is an example of a text in which I make extensive use of various kinds of synonyms.

It awaits you at every corner.
Ambushes you at every turn.
Pursues you to annihilation.
Pollutes and mars your sleep.
It overpowers your thoughts.
Quickens and deranges your imagination.
Inundates your consciousness.
Electrifies, nay, inflames your nights.
It is there – all set, fraught.
In position.
Alert.
Watchful.
It is only a matter of time.

- *Reiteration:* This is a strategy that I especially like and use extensively. Reiteration is designed to emphasize a meaning, a theme, an idea, a rhythm, or an experience. The element that is repeated can be a key word, a lexical base, a collocation (two or more words that normally go together), an idea, or more. To me, such repetition carries a lot of meaning because it signals to the addressees that the reiterated element is significant, directing them to pay special attention to it.

Here is an example in which I used reiteration to explain the notion of a precipitating event. I created this text for my personal blog to convey the trauma that my family and I had experienced on account of the car accident I wrote about in the beginning of this book.

A trigger event – it blasts inward through locked doors, drawn blinds, and closed windows. It splits the mortar, breaks down the walls, rips out the foundations. It surges in like a torrent, tearing, sweeping everything in its path. Leaving ruins and detritus in its wake.

- *Resonance, quotations, allusions:* These strategies involve lexical referencing of a person, an event, or another work, and they can be either overt or subtle. At issue are intertextual links between the content at hand and other stories that compel the audience to engage with the former by virtue of its connection with the latter.

In such instances, the processing is contingent on the addressees' familiarity with other salient contexts and semiotic frameworks, which is essential to achieve the desired effect. It is important to keep in mind that the content alluded to can be a story, a picture, a movie, an incident, an episode, an advertisement, and so on – in other words, any content that our audience knows or has heard about in any format.

- *Descriptive verbs:* These lexical elements are located on a value scale from positive to neutral to negative. Thus, if I write about someone that he "presumes to explain," will your response be the same as if I write that he "endeavors to explain"? The answer is "definitely no," because my choice of the expressive means reflects my own perception regarding the individual referred to, and also signals to the addressees that they should adopt my point of view.

- *Active vs. passive voice and related variations:* The use of active as opposed to passive structures reflects the narrator's stance regarding personal responsibility for the action described. Thus, the sentence "The glass broke," rather than "I broke the glass," implies that the speaker does not admit responsibility for the outcome, as though the glass broke of its own accord. In the second sentence, the blame for the broken glass is clearly acknowledged. Or if you read about someone that he "considers himself" or that he "is considered" – can you discern the difference in the effect stemming from the choice of phrasing?

Opting for active verbs serves an additional goal. Such expressions can often create the sense that something is happening, that events occur one after another sequentially, that there is movement: I got up, went, met, returned... Accordingly, when you tell a story and wish to set a dynamic rhythm, it is advisable to use active verbs.

- Singular vs. plural: Another element that should not be taken lightly, although it may seem innocuous at first glance, is the choice between the singular and the plural forms of a noun or a pronoun. The saying "success has many fathers, but failure is an orphan" didn't emerge out of thin air. In many instances, similar to the case with active and passive verbs, it points to the extent to which the speaker is prepared to admit responsibility for what is being said, for example, "We have erred," as opposed to "I have erred."

In many other instances, by using the plural, the speaker stresses that the scenario described is common, for example, when she presents a personal problem as one that is relevant to many other people or when he discusses a frequent or ubiquitous phenomenon. This usage involves generalization designed to expand the scope of an event beyond the specific circumstances in which it occurred and thus render it relevant to a group, a society, or even humanity as a whole.

Structural-stylistic tools

Each of us has a distinctive style, which we should cherish, as it expresses our unique voice and is our key to achieving authenticity and credibility. That said, several rules of thumb need to be kept in mind and followed when attempting to build a good story. This is essential for any goal-oriented writing and to filter out irrelevant facts.

- Brevity and selectivity: Pascal once concluded a letter to

a friend with an apology that he had not had the time to write briefly. Similarly, a good story can say a lot with relatively few words. Writing concisely takes a lot of time, but the investment is worthwhile. One of the ways to achieve brevity is by loading a word with several meanings, for example through using tropes and metaphor, as well as polysemous terms. Also, in telling a story, we need to choose very carefully the episodes to include in it – the right moments, as it were.

But what are these "right moments"?

McKee maintains that the story of each character, event, or incident contains an enormous range of possibilities. The choice of the "right moments" depends on the narrator's ability to see the uniqueness of the character and the important and meaningful aspects of the occurrences, and to build a rich and satisfying narrative around these focal points. A narrator's main challenge, then, is to find only those moments that encapsulate and recreate a whole life, even though the story presents only a small part of it, the moments whose description will open before your audience a view on an entire world.

A story can be very short and nonetheless convey a lot of meaning. A good example is the shortest story of all, attributed – rightfully or not – to Ernest Hemingway.

"For sale: baby shoes, never worn."

The text is extremely concise, and therein lies its power. The story creates a gap and invites the audience to fill it, thus involving them in the narrative and inducing them to own it, so to speak.

- *Embedded questions*: One of the strategies that I always recommend to my clients is using questions. This works well in just about every story we tell, irrespective of the format or the platform that we choose to use for it. However, this element is especially useful in a presentation and for lecturers. When I work one-on-one with a client on building a presentation, I usually present an excerpt twice: once with questions integrated into the text and once without. In this way, I vividly demonstrate how questions contribute to the effectiveness of the presentation.

You know what?

Check this out for yourself. Go over the questions that I have incorporated throughout this book and see how they propel its "plot" forward.

A good tip to follow in any learning and implementation process is to try to figure out what affects you, why, and how, and to pay attention and study how things are done and not just what is being said.

Why do questions have such power?

Because they push the story onward, engage the audience, and, if used correctly, can enhance attention by building up anticipatory tension and suspense. Just like a good story itself. The secret of their effect is in compelling the addressee to think about an answer, even if the question itself is rhetorical. Rhetorical questions are, in general, an excellent way to give the addressees the feeling that they are taking part in the narrated events – which, of course, they are not. Sometimes we need these kinds of tricks as well.

In one of my workshops on building a story-based presentation, I use numerous questions to induce the audience to come up with automatic answers, which I subsequently refute, one by one. This is essentially a ping-pong game: I ask a leading question, get an answer that I was waiting for, and then reject it and provide one of my own. This strategy never fails to surprise my audience, flout their expectations, and gradually also create tension – when the participants get the meaning of the game and realize that the questions were not nearly as innocuous as they seemed at the outset. This is also a great way to keep the audience alert and enthralled.

- *Intertextuality*: The subject of context in general, and of intertextuality in particular, is of great importance in strategic storytelling. Indeed, while the decoding process whereby the addressee derives meaning from text is universal, its outcomes depend on the audience – their knowledge, their ability to draw inferences, as well as the cultural, social, and community-specific conditions that they are exposed to. The processing of a story requires the addressees to fill in the gaps by adding elements in accordance with their own knowledge and understanding, and the way they do this depends on how they conceive of the information relayed and on the intra- and extra-textual links they establish during the decoding process.

Illustration

- *Verbal illustration*: The purpose of this strategy is to promote visualization. Illustrating a concept or a notion verbally, through phraseology and description, impels the audience to form a mental image of the content being conveyed. An effective example of this technique, and one that I like to use, is Apple's iPod advertisement that I introduced earlier. As you might recall, in their promotion of the audio device, the company does not extol its superior qualities, but instead it represents the main advantage vividly in a single sentence: "A thousand songs in your pocket." By contrast, Apple's competitors promoted similar products by detailing the features in terms of mega- and gigabytes and so on, elements that a rank-and-file consumer cannot easily process or understand. In other words, a good story can make recondite data lucid and comprehensible.

- *Visual illustration*: This rubric encompasses all visual representation, both cognition- and emotion-oriented, that can be appropriately used as aids in a story, such as images, graphics, infographics, and the like. I could define this type of strategy in three words: single-frame story.

By means of a single-frame story, it is possible to establish what is known as "rational anchoring," for example, by presenting evidence in graphs or displaying data as infographics, since this kind of information is more easily conveyed and comprehended through such modes than in a textual format. At the same time, visual representation can function as shortcuts to emotions, nostalgic memories, myths, codes, and cultural symbols – primarily if the frame employed involves metaphors and creates connotative links.

Below is an ad that was posted in our neighborhood shopping center.

OlgaRybtsova/Thinkstock by Getty Images (Reconstruction)

By choosing the image of Mary Poppins, the advertiser manages to evoke a wealth of associations. The picture encapsulates all the wondrous qualities ascribed to the character of Mary Poppins – efficiency, responsibility, motherly care, and more. Through a single image, it not only communicates to the addressee a tremendous amount of salient information, but also arouses emotion rooted in part in nostalgia and longing for the pure world of childhood.

How many words would we need to express all this

information without this image?

But wait... What about those who haven't seen the movie or who don't even know the story? Unlikely as it might seem, there are such people. Well, in that case, we would be relying on the contextual schema, on the assumption that our addressees process stories within the setting of the culture, era, and society in which they live. As regards Mary Poppins, I presume that the vast majority of the target audience – in this case parents – are familiar with both the character and the story behind it, and are thus capable of processing the advertisement as intended by its author.

- *Illustration using voice and body language*: These strategies, which I relegate to the extra-textual dimension, involve the use of voice, music, silence, intonation, and body language, the latter including eye contact, provided such means can be appropriately employed to aid the story and enhance its effectiveness. While at first glance this set of illustrative tools appear as extra-textual, they are in fact an inseparable part of any story.

This kind of illustration is relevant mostly when telling a story in front of an audience, including business meetings, staff meetings, lectures, and presentations, but also in clips and photographs.

As concerns intonation, one must remember that a superlative sentence such as "I was excited and jumped for joy" cannot be said quietly and monotonically, with a woebegone facial expression. Enunciated in this manner, an utterance of this kind creates a dissonance in the addressee's mind and arouses incredulity vis-à-vis the narrator and the narrated. The same is true for music. Imagine that you are screening a promotion clip that depicts your clients as energetic, spirited, and dynamic, but the background music is soft and soothing. In such a case, the subconscious impact of the music is at odds with the overt message, giving rise to disharmony.

What about silence?

In my opinion, silence is greatly underrated as a rhetorical tool. Try to punctuate your story with pauses, each akin to a rest in a climactic part of a motet, and observe the enormous power of what is not there. In his essay "Revealment and Concealment in Language" (1975), H. N. Bialik notes that language protects man from facing the existential abyss, and that in this regard words are not much more than a distraction.

By incorporating silences into your stories, you can propel your listeners to the brink of this abyss and compel them to look down, as it were. Try it, and you will see how quickly they will strive to fill the silence with words.

To sum up, to inject life into your content, it is advisable to use voice and body language. In this way, you can transform your story into a living thing. Endow it with additional dimensions, and you will give it depth. But of course, everything is better in moderation. It's not as if you were putting on a Shakespeare play in Stratford-upon-Avon.

So if you have already understood that your choice of expressive means must always be motivated and informed, that the same thing can be told in a variety of ways, and that your storytelling decisions must never be random...

And if, at this point, you agree that stories cannot be neutral or "naïve," as some of us might have thought, and that storytelling is a practice that is inherently goal-oriented and rife with covert agendas, either conscious or incidental...

And if by now you have realized that every story has a deep layer that manifests bias, whether in its overall organization, style, linguistic choices, lexicon, visualization, and other aspects, then you surely understand that when you are telling a story, whether personal, organizational, or business-oriented, whether written, oral, or visual, and whether one-on-one, before a live audience, or online – you must be able to tell your story in such a way that it will reach your audience and promote your agendas and goals. And if you learn to do this well, you will find yourself in possession of a strategic tool with a powerful rhetorical impact, one that you can use for a variety of purposes, in life, at work, and in business.

So what now? Now we can really get to work!

In the next section, I will present a guideline for building effective stories, stories that can help you further your agendas and goals irrespective of the platform you choose to use.

O. G. GOAZ

14

The Devil Is in the Details

The method expounded in EFFECTIVE STORYTELLING STEP BY STEP is based on an assumption that the tools I introduce and discuss in this book can help promote agendas and goals – in life, at work, and in business.

In other words, what I am offering you here is a tool kit for understanding storytelling as a goal-oriented practice, one that requires you to think, first and foremost, how to benefit from the way you tell your stories – which we all tell anyway.

Our framework for building an effective story comprises three main layers.

The first layer contains all the ingredients that a story must incorporate in order to be worthy of being told – the components that throughout this book we have referred to as schemas for effective storytelling, the narrative staples, seasoning, and the like.

The second layer includes what Labov (1972) calls evaluative devices; that is, the cognitive means designed to persuade the audience by appealing to their rational, logical thinking, and the solicitation strategies that target emotion through stylistic rhetorical elements including reiteration, connotation, and tropes, as well as deliberate choices related to structure, organization, style, and various illustrative means.

The third layer contains the agenda and goals that we seek to advance through our story.

To learn to apply the methodology promoted by EFFECTIVE STORYTELLING STEP BY STEP I suggest a small exercise. Choose a story that you like, be it a Facebook post, a YouTube clip, an advertisement, or even one of the stories that I have told you here. Then try to critically scrutinize the story you selected in light of the following questions:

- Why did I choose this particular story?
- What in the story did I find convincing / appealing / moving / relevant?
- Can I discern the author's position?
- Why is the story relayed in this particular way and not another?

Think about the way the story is constructed, about the process through which the preferred meaning is negotiated, and the role therein of the style, characters, plot, tone, and linguistic choices.

After you have identified the meaning, which, as we have already seen, lies for the most part in the story's hidden layer rather than being overtly stated, you need to establish how this meaning is concealed within the language. You must pay attention to the order in which the events are relayed, note the author's linguistic choices, and identify the informative parts that at first appear neutral – although they are inherently biased.

Researchers explain that understanding how symbols within a content unit propel us towards a shared meaning can be achieved by following two analytical axes: paradigmatic and syntactic relations in the text.

The examination of syntactic relations involves identifying the connections between the various signs within the story that create meaning, or in other words, identifying the way its constituent elements are arranged. The premise is that a different ordering would have dictated a different meaning. The analysis of paradigmatic relations, on the other hand, involves scrutinizing linguistic choices and inferring why the author chose them, since the use of different expressive means would have changed the meaning of the story.

As part of the exercise, you also need to single out and mark the author's poetic and rhetoric choices in the story and identify key words, reiteration, rhyme, leading questions, elements revealing bias, and other components discussed earlier.

At the same time, you must pay attention to the intertextual links connecting the story to more widely familiar narratives, myths, and symbols that encapsulate and condense information and thereby serve as shortcuts to goal-oriented processing and influencing the addressee. Thus, for example, allusions to the Cinderella fairytale or to the myth of David and Goliath will give rise in our minds to different analogies that will, in turn, pattern the story according to its genre and thus dictate the intended meaning. We can compare this process to pressing an imaginary button in our addressee's brain that makes the processing mechanism operate in accordance with the author's intentions.

And finally, try to establish from which universes of discourse the author chose the expressive means, and what meanings and imaginative worlds have been conjured as a result. For example, in a discourse universe of "war," words like "occupation" will frequently appear; the "Olympic games" universe will use such images as "passing the torch"; the "competition" universe will contain terms like "winning," and so on and so forth.

If used correctly, all these elements will ensure that your stories will pass under the radar and will be accepted without resistance, because most people consume stories without analyzing them.

And now let's learn to implement in practice the theoretical knowledge we have accrued thus far.

15

Putting the Storytelling Puzzle Together

As I have already said, for me, storytelling out of awareness is a permanent state of mind. What I mean is that my stories tell themselves – according to a set of guidelines, in line with popular schemas, and, up to a point, using various tools to promote agendas and goals. This is mainly because I am always consciously aware of these rules and elements, such that they have become part of my everyday life.

That is partly by virtue of my education and over twenty years of professional experience (as a communications advisor, spokeswoman, and public relations expert). But it's also because I rely on storytelling in my personal life, mainly to help my children grow up in harmony with themselves, and at work, to help my clients to promote their agendas and goals. For all these reasons I have developed an almost complete awareness of the effectiveness of my storytelling choices and their impact on and implications for others. However, a person who does not live and breathe stories on a daily basis as I do can use the framework that I introduce and set out in this book as a good starting point, as well as scaffolding for safe climbing – so go ahead, tell it right!

For maximum benefit, I strongly advise you to first read all the steps that I enumerate here, then go over the example presented in the next chapter, which features stories that I have constructed by following this template, and only after that to retrace your steps and complete the exercise in this chapter by filling out the rubrics based on your own story.

First, decide what you want to tell.

Recall that a predominant element in our stories is seasoning: do not invent, find! You must find your story (which need not be about something that has happened directly to you), and this will largely ensure its authenticity and credibility.

Recall also that your story must be marked with integrity, in the sense that you are at liberty to tell it and that it expresses your credo and values.

Recall, finally, that there is nothing wrong in choosing a story that reveals your weaknesses. Remember: it is by acknowledging your human vulnerability that you invest your story with power – look at me and behold yourselves. This ensures, almost by default, that your story contains an element of universality, since the minute you show that you are weak, you also point to weaknesses shared by most humans. It is as if you were asking, "Did you really believe that you are an exception?"

Either way, your storytelling choices must be conscious and deliberate. To achieve this kind of awareness, I suggest that you ask yourself several questions, the answers to which will help you at a later stage to promote your agenda and goals. The guidelines are presented below as a template, for you to fill in the content. This will be your first attempt at storytelling under my guidance.

I must remind you, however, that before completing this exercise, you should read through to the end of the next chapter!

Step 1: Factual Framework

Write down your facts: the events and other information that you want to tell about and include in your story. Do not add interpretation or remarks that point to your attitude towards the content, and do not use any figures of speech, descriptions, or rhetorical elements that are discussed in the chapter on agenda-promoting strategies.

Here, write down your story in a nutshell, producing a kind of synopsis that answers the question, "What is the story about?"

Note that your outline must be concise and precise, listing only the essential elements of the events and information that will figure in the story.

_____

_____

_____

_____

_____

_____

_____

_____

_____

_____

_____

_____

_____

_____

_____

_____

Anchoring

Here write down the "five Ws": Who? What? When? Where? Why?

Note that although it may sometimes seem that not all of the "five Ws" are relevant to your story, it is a good idea to write down all the answers anyway, even if at a later point you will decide not to incorporate them into the story.

_____

_____

_____

_____

_____

_____

_____

What is the precipitating event in your story?

Here write down the change, problem, paradoxical occurrence or element, complication, or obstacle. The question that should guide you in this task is, "What happened?"

Note that not every story must have an event of supreme importance, in the absolute sense; yet there must be an occurrence that carries significance for the story's characters.

_____

_____

_____

_____

_____

_____

_____

_____

_____

What are the outcomes? How is the complication resolved?

Here you need to present a solution – the way out of the impasse or the way to surmount the obstacle.

Note that, as explained in the chapter on the story's constituent elements, the resolution need not lead to a happy ending. The solution can be either good or bad, constructive or misguided.

_____

_____

_____

_____

_____

_____

_____

_____

_____

_____

Step 2 – Foundation

What is the purpose of the story?

What objective do you wish to achieve through your story? The purpose must be clear and well defined.

If your purpose is marketing or selling a product or a service, you must keep in mind that once people realize this, they usually stop listening. This kind of story, therefore, must be especially well constructed.

Purpose:

_____

_____

_____

Who is your target audience?

Recall that a story must be relevant for its intended addressees. Thus, being able to tell a story is not enough; it is essential to know how to tell the right story, one that will engage the target audience. The name of the game here is salience. Remember: it is always easier to tell a story anchored in values already embraced by your audience than to persuade them to adopt a belief or a principle, or to accept a value that may contravene those they already have. In other words, you need to know your audience and to be prepared to change your story if you feel that it doesn't resonate with their perceptions.

The audience:

How do you propose to capture your audience's attention and arouse their interest?

One way to elicit engagement is by structuring your story to create tension. If you can puzzle your addressees, make them anticipate events, or make them feel uncertain, you can "capture" your audience and keep them wondering: How will the story end? What happens next? What is in store for the character? Always remember that as long as your readers are uncertain about how the plot will proceed or what will happen to the protagonist they have by now come to care about, you've got a captive audience.

Focus and interest:

_____

_____

_____

_____

_____

_____

_____

_____

_____

What elements in your story will elicit engagement?

In order to engage the audience, your story must arouse some kind of emotion. What component(s) of your story are designed to serve this purpose? How will you establish an affective link with your addressees?

American poet and author Maya Angelou said, "I've learned that people will forget what you said, people will forget what you did, but people will never forget how you made them feel." A story must evoke feelings, for at least two reasons. First, it is your story's affective elements that will ensure that people will evaluate it positively, because, as Maya Angelou perspicaciously notes, people are deeply influenced by the effects of an experience. Second – and mainly insofar as business storytelling is concerned – you must keep in mind that the reasons that people buy products are rooted in emotion, even though they usually rationalize their decisions logically.

Last but not least, as already shown, in order to engage our addressees, our story needs to include lacunae – gaps and pauses – allowing the audience to fill them in. In this way, they get the impression that they have reached independent conclusions and thus feel less like passive bystanders and more like active participants. In some cases, this strategy may induce the addressees to adopt the story, so to say, and make it their own, without compromising their understanding of its import.

Engagement:

_____

_____

_____

_____

_____

_____

_____

_____

What do your addressees stand to gain by listening to your story?

A story must benefit the listeners in some substantive way, through its deep and hidden meaning and through enriching their understanding of reality. In a sense, a story needs to operate in two dimensions: while recounting a personal experience, it must at the same time convey a universal message.

Remember that a story that produces experiential knowledge goes a long way. Yet I must warn the reader that often even this is not enough. It is true that good storytelling is couched in distraction and diversion, but when the pleasurable sensations subside and the enjoyment wanes, the listeners go home empty-handed, and all your hard work is wasted. So, despite what I said above, and notwithstanding Maya Angelou's comment, over and above the diversion that our story provides, our task is to leave an imprint on our listeners' minds, make a point, and give them something valuable and meaningful, something that they will treasure and cherish.

This is also based on my own experience. Once I heard a lecture that was fascinating, funny, and highly enjoyable. After a few days, however, I realized that the recollection no longer brought a smile to my lips, and I asked myself, "What did I actually gain from the lecture?" My answer was, "Nothing." To be sure, I had had a very good time – which is not to be taken lightly, because many lectures I have attended weren't even entertaining. What I am trying to say is that, once you've managed to get your audience to enjoy your story, why not aim higher? Why not try and leave a mark on their consciousness, give them something of value?

The value your addressees will derive from your story:

_____

_____

_____

_____

_____

_____

_____

_____

_____

_____

Step 3 – Schema

Study the schemas for effective storytelling and decide if you've got a story in your arsenal that fits one of them. An advantage of using a schema is that stories that become popular and engage the addressees usually follow one. To remind you of the possible options, below are the most successful schemas.

The **Misarrangement** category includes the schemas of *Resonance* and *Inversion*. This pattern can be suitable if your story includes a surprise element or if it jumbles up a known story.

"Hot" Stories, including the *News*, *Context*, and *Celebrities* schemas, are helpful if your story contains some new information that is related to a topic currently on the public agenda or if it is about a celebrity of any kind.

Discovery, including the *Research* and *"From my own experience"* schemas, can be used mainly for stories centered on human nature, health issues, and lifestyle.

Against All Odds, including the *Cinderella* and *The underdog* schemas, is suitable for stories about business ventures or any story relaying a hero's struggle against more powerful forces.

Alluring Stories, including the *"I have a secret!"* and *Scandals* schemas, are excellent for gossip, voyeuristic episodes, and exposing someone or something.

Mutual Responsibility, including the *"Friends – to our aid!"* and *"For the good of the public"* schemas, is suitable for appealing to the public for support or endorsement and for any story meant as a warning.

Humor, including the *"This is really funny!"* and *Practical jokes* schemas, can be used for any story that will bring a smile to your audience's faces.

The Classic Story, which contains *The hero's journey* schema, is helpful for telling a story in which the protagonist undertakes a quest.

It is important that your choice of schema is conscious and informed. For example, if you want to talk about a small company that is competing against giant corporations, the schema that would fit the bill the best is the underdog, provided your story aligns with this paradigm. On the other hand, if a story is sad, then a humorous rendering, such as a practical joke, would be inappropriate in most cases.

You must keep in mind that, in many instances, a story can fit more than one schema, and there is nothing wrong with that. Thus, for example, the hero's journey paradigm is user-friendly and is frequently chosen to promote business stories, often in combination with other schemas.

That said, if your story doesn't seem to fit into any of the paradigms suggested above, it's fine too. As I already explained, one would be unwise to discard a good story only because it does not align with a popular schema. While the paradigms listed above can indeed make a story viral, there are many stories that do not precisely or unambiguously fit into any single pattern but have nevertheless been proven highly effective and have even become viral.

Step 4 – Narrative Glue

At this point, all the puzzle pieces need to be put together by means of our narrative choices and evaluation elements so as to form the big picture. Narrative scholars have argued that the common feature of all narratives is that they constitute a sequence leading to some sort of an outcome. In other words, for a text to be considered narrative, all the events included in it must be filtered, arranged, attached to one another, and perceived by the audience as significant. To produce a text that meets these criteria, we must link together all the events and information. If we follow a schema, this task becomes easier, for all that's left for us to do is connect the narrative elements according to that schema.

In the literature, this stage is termed "the narrative glue," referring to the elements that connect the facts and data into a sequential plot that is worth being told. In order to do this, you must make sure that your story follows a narrative sequence that leads to an outcome, or in other words, that it incorporates a plot that invests the sequence of events narrated with meaning, internal logic, and import.

To ensure that you are on the right path, that is, that you have connected all the facts and wrapped the grid that emerged as a result in all the trappings of a plot, you need to check that your story meets the three conditions listed below.

- *A beginning, a middle, and an end.* Jean-Luc Godard said that "a story should have a beginning, a middle, and an end, but not necessarily in that order." Accordingly, when I build for my clients a presentation or a lecture that includes what I call "an unforgettable story," I almost invariably suggest that they start... with a climactic point. This is one way to capture the audience.

- *The narrator or the angle.*

- *One or several characters who impact or are impacted by an event.*

From here, you can proceed to the next stage only if you have checked off all three elements. If one of these parameters is missing but the story is constructed according to one of the schemas, this may do as well. However, if you are not using a schema for successful storytelling, I suggest you ensure that all the three criteria are met. In this case, you might need to try and change the story, adding the missing elements.

Step 5 – Import

What is the point that makes your story worth telling? The question to be discussed here concerns what the addressees will take away after hearing your story.

Remember to note down the lesson, the insight, the understanding, the statement, or the broader / universal significance of your story. The coda, which signals the conclusion of the story and brings us back to the present, is the point that must encapsulate the story's import.

The import:

_____

_____

_____

_____

_____

_____

_____

_____

_____

_____

Step 6 – Evaluative Elements

Now that the story is essentially ready, reread it and check whether it contains narrative elements required for promoting your agenda and goals. That is, see whether it incorporates the various evaluative elements that will prompt the addressees to follow you all the way. If not, try to add some or to change the story to include the tools described in the chapter on advancing agenda and goals. Remember: evaluative elements are the building materials that enable us to take the story to where we want our audience to follow it.

In this way you can implement the theoretical guidelines in practice. When you are reading your story, ask yourself the following questions:

Have you incorporated rational anchors? We are talking here about such information as time, place, dates, numbers, and data.

Have you incorporated into your story rhetorical tools? These are shortcuts to people's emotions, empathy, understanding, and acceptance, and are consequently going to be an effective means for persuading and influencing your addressees. Such tools include metaphors, rhyming, reiteration, links to symbols, rhetorical questions, imagery, personification, connotation, evocation, and resonance.

Is your story showing rather than telling the audience what you wish to convey?

Have you illustrated the content of your story with salient and appropriate examples?

This is not the time to let up! This stage is the most important one. Go back to Chapter 11 and review all the elements that can help you invest your story with color, drama, and tension, and to evoke engagement, attention, and so on. Check where you can add or remove content, change the wording, and so on.

Step 7 – Writing the Story

Write the complete version of your story here. Do this only after you have finished reading through the end of the next chapter.

_____

_____

_____

_____

_____

_____

_____

_____

_____

_____

_____

_____

_____

_____

_____

_____

_____

_____

_____

_____

_____

_____

_____

_____

_____

_____

_____

_____

_____

_____

_____

_____

_____

_____

_____

Now that your story is ready, read it over again and polish it up. When you feel that it is good, that it is worthy of being told, run it past another person or several people, those whose opinion you value and rely on. Discuss with that person whether the story successfully conveys the message that it was intended to get across, if it is interesting, and if it attains your objective.

If the story needs to be transposed from written text to a visual medium, you must illustrate and "translate" the wording to a storyboard, to visuals that tell it and convey its message. If it is an image, like a still picture, try to create one that tells the story in a single frame.

Can this be done at all?

Certainly! Remember: One picture is worth a thousand words!

However, this is theory. Here is an example of a single-frame story that I saw on a notice board in our neighborhood. The text translates as:

"Do you need a life preserver?"

"Closet organizing and decluttering"

Ryan McV/Thinkstock by Getty Images (Reconstruction)

Note how clear and eloquent is the image of a tidal wave, made up of clothes, that is about to engulf everything. This picture demonstrates that it is feasible to fit a story into a single frame and include in it all the elements discussed by Labov and McKee: a protagonist, an event or a predicament, imagery, import, and more.

So please remember: A story can be relayed in a post, a

clip, or an evocative image (like the babysitter advertisement with Mary Poppins), a video script, an advertisement, a presentation, a lecture, and more. The guided practice offered here uses language because words are the foundation for building a story, which can subsequently be conveyed in any medium and on any platform you choose.

If this platform is not accessible to your addressees, as the next step, you must translate and transpose your story to any other medium or platform that you decide to use.

As one who does this routinely as a job, I can share with you my personal experience: One can achieve excellent results by building a presentation composed of images based on a story in a text format.

Step 8 – Sharing Your Story

Now that your story is ready, all that is left is to decide where to tell it.

Irrespective of the setting in which you plan to recount it – while chatting with your friends, in a meeting, or in front of an audience, be it in a conference room or a lecture hall – first of all, get a mirror and tell it several times to yourself. Pay attention how you act your story out. Incorporate eye-contact, intonation, and body language that are appropriate in the circumstances. You can even film yourself and then watch the video recording.

In any event, make sure that your story is not "flat," because it is not enough to create only the text. Find ways to play out parts of your story using voice (emphasis, volume manipulation, silent pauses), as well as hand gestures and body posture. Needless to say, all these means must be used with discretion; after all, your purpose is to illustrate and accentuate the content, not to stage a Broadway production – always keep that in mind.

If your story is in the form of text, published either on paper or digitally, as a post, article, or advertisement, recall the discussion on how to illustrate a story visually, through images or infographics that can significantly enhance its effectiveness.

And the most important thing to remember is that the devil is in the details!

16

From Theory to Practice

The following exercise will give you a glimpse behind the scenes: I will explain how I used the above guiding questions to build an effective story.

This is essentially the inductive method of teaching, using an example to show how to implement the theoretical rubrics in practice and extrapolate the case at hand to other possible scenarios.

I chose a true story for my example, something that happened to me in the beginning of 2016, during the so-called "Intifada of individuals," a wave of violence in the Israeli-Palestinian conflict marked by numerous stabbings and other terrorist acts perpetrated by individuals acting alone or in league with a trusted relative.

> Last night I found myself alone in a taxi share going from Modi'in to Jerusalem on Highway 443. The driver was listening to the popular Israeli music radio station Galgalatz, operated by Israel Defense Forces

Radio. I paid the fee and sat down in the front seat next to the driver. At the last stop before we left Modi'in, after which the road meanders for a long time among Arab villages, another passenger entered the taxi. He paid and took the seat behind the driver. A few minutes later, the driver and the passenger struck up a conversation. In Arabic. The time was eight p.m. It was already dark. The highway we were driving on crossed the separation fence between the contested Israeli-Palestinian areas. And here I was: in a taxi, alone with two men talking to each other in Arabic. I felt my heart pounding in my chest. I felt my face getting hotter and hotter. The driver's phone rang. He turned off the radio and answered in Arabic. Every so often I discerned the word "Palestine." And again "Palestine." I started feeling nauseated. I was holding an umbrella that I had bought in Germany. I clasped it tight. After all, I had been a self-defense instructor in the IDF. I swallowed hard. I started thinking of possible scenarios. What if the driver suddenly swerves off the road and heads toward a Palestinian village? There are two of them. I am alone. I tried to figure out which way the accursed door opened – the one with the long handle. I dialed my home number. Not that I wanted to alarm anyone. In a weak voice I told my husband that I was in a taxi share going from Modi'in to Jerusalem. Just to ensure that someone knew. I rang off and my battery went dead. "Idiot." The tension rose. I saw that we were approaching the army checkpoint. I said to the driver, "Stop. I need to throw up." I wasn't even sure if I was lying or telling the truth. The driver said, "I can't stop here. Only after the checkpoint." I thought to myself, what if he doesn't stop? My heart beat even faster now – if that was at all possible. Should I do something? Should I say something to the soldiers? What could I say? The driver and the passenger hadn't done anything wrong; their only transgression was talking in their native language, Arabic. I stood up in the moving taxi. "Stop!" I shouted inwardly and held my breath until the vehicle slowed down to a stop. I got out. I bent over the guardrail, pretending to throw up. The driver waited with the door open. I straightened up and said to him, "Go." He said, "It's a shame, we are almost there." I said to him, "Go. I am sorry. Go." He drove off, and I felt so ashamed.

Précis

One evening, the protagonist takes a taxi share going from Modi'in to Jerusalem via Highway 443, a road that crosses the separation fence between the contested Israeli-Palestinian areas and runs among numerous Arab villages. On the way, she discovers that the driver and the only other passenger are Arabs. Halfway through the trip, when the taxi passes a military check post, the protagonist asks the driver to pull up at the side of the road and gets out.

Orientation

Who? The protagonist is an Israeli woman; the other characters are the driver and a passenger, both Arab men.

What are the circumstances? A ride in a taxi share.

When? An evening during the "Intifada of the individuals."

Where? From Modi'in to Jerusalem via Highway 443.

Why? Returning home.

Complication

The protagonist discovers that the driver and the only other passenger are Arabs.

Resolution

The protagonist gets out of the taxi halfway through the trip.

Objective

To show that I, the narrator of the story and author of this book, know how to tell a story that would move the audience, foster identification, and create strong engagement – as part of the campaign for promoting and marketing the Hebrew edition of EFFECTIVE STORYTELLING STEP BY STEP.

The addressees

Potential buyers of the book EFFECTIVE STORYTELLING STEP BY STEP in the preliminary online sale.

Arousing the addressees' attention and interest
This is achieved in two ways. The first is creating tension and gradually raising its level. The second is implementing the *Context* schema within the category of "Hot" stories with the backdrop of the "Intifada of the individuals" in Israel and the consequent stressful atmosphere in the country.

Eliciting engagement
This is achieved by revealing the protagonist's vulnerability. In this case, the story relays an individual experience that sheds light on the complexities of Israeli reality at the time. An additional tool for eliciting engagement is incorporating questions into the text.

Value for the addressees
Providing diversion (in the Pascalian sense of this term – remember?), creating order in chaos, giving expression to the addressees' fears and apprehensions through the protagonist's experiences during her journey.

Schema

The hero's journey from the **Classic Story** category; the *Context* schema.

Narrative glue

Last night I found myself alone in a taxi share going from Modi'in to Jerusalem on Highway 443. At the last stop another passenger entered the taxi. After we had left Modi'in, the driver and the passenger started talking to each other in Arabic. At a certain point, the driver's phone rang, and he answered in Arabic, using the word "Palestine" in the conversation. When we arrived at a military check post, I asked the driver to stop the taxi, on the pretext that I had to vomit. The driver stopped after the check post and let me get off. After pretending to vomit, I told the driver to continue without me. The driver tried to persuade me to get back in the car, but I refused.

Checklist for narrative components

✓ Is there a beginning, a middle, and an end?

✓ Is there a narrator or a point of view?

✓ Are there characters impacting or being impacted by the key event?

Evaluative elements

(1) Last night I found myself (2) alone (3) in a taxi share (4) going from Modi'in to Jerusalem on (5) Highway 443. The driver was listening to (6) the popular Israeli music radio station Galgalatz, operated by Israel Defense Forces Radio.	(1) Rational anchor – time. (2) Intra-narrative objective – building a rationale. (3) Intra-narrative objective – preparing for what is to come next – the arrival of another passenger. (4) Rational anchor – spatial deixis. (5) Intertextual contextualization

I paid the fee and sat down (7) in the front seat next to the driver. (8) At the last stop before we left Modi'in, after which the road meanders among Arab villages for a long time, another passenger entered the taxi. He paid (9) and took the seat behind the driver. A few minutes later, the driver and the passenger struck up a conversation. (10) In Arabic. (11) The time was eight p.m. It was already dark. The highway we were driving on crossed the separation fence between the contested Israeli-Palestinian areas. (12) And here I was: in a taxi, alone with two men talking to each other in Arabic. (13) I felt my heart pounding in my chest. I felt my face getting hotter and hotter. The driver's phone rang. (14) He turned off the radio and answered in Arabic. Every so often I discerned (15) the word "Palestine." And again "Palestine." (16) I started feeling nauseated.

(17) I was holding an umbrella that I had bought in

– requires processing based on socio-cultural knowledge. (6) Socio-cultural context, attests to the driver's reliability. (7) Creating a mental picture. (8) Socio-cultural context – creates the understanding that, from that point on, no additional passengers can enter the vehicle, and thus that the situation in the taxi cannot be changed. (9) Illustrating the situation in the taxi by creating a mental picture. (10) Socio-cultural context designed to build tension. (11) Reiteration with the purpose of building tension. (12) Reiteration designed to build tension – socio-cultural context. (13) Emotive tools – the showing of fear together with telling about it. (14) A means for advancing the plot that is retrospectively understood to be the story's turning point. (15) Reiteration for the purposes of emphasis – socio-cultural context. (16) The telling – an element employed later on, when it becomes clear that the nausea is not motion sickness. (17) An element used to create the

Germany.

(18) I clasped it tight. (19) After all, I had been a self-defense instructor in the IDF. (20) I swallowed hard. I started thinking of possible scenarios. What if the driver suddenly swerves off the road and heads toward a Palestinian village? (21) There are two of them. I am alone.

I tried to figure out (22) which way the accursed door opened – the one with the long handle. I dialed my home number. Not that I wanted to alarm anyone.

(23) In a weak voice I told my husband that I was in a taxi share going from Modi'in to Jerusalem. (24) Just to ensure that someone knew. I rang off and my battery went dead. (25) "Idiot." (26) The tension rose. I saw that we were approaching the army checkpoint. I said to the driver, "Stop. I need to throw up." (27) I wasn't even sure if I was lying or telling the truth. The driver said, "I can't stop here. Only after the

image of a weapon – the mention of Germany alludes to the sturdiness and high quality of the item in question. (18) Alludes to the intention to use the item if required. (19) Justifies the intention, rather ambitious, to try to fight two men with only an umbrella for a weapon. (20) The showing – indicates fear. (21) Reiteration for the purposes of emphasis, stressing the grammatical difference between masculine and feminine in the Hebrew second-person verb form. This exacerbates the tension by adding a gender dimension to the already present political-nationalist facet. (22) A means to create the feeling of being trapped. (23) The word "weak" carries a double meaning: the voice can be kept intentionally low so as not to be heard, but can also be feeble unintentionally, pointing to the speaker's general weakness. (24) Projects despair. (25) Inner dialogue presented as a direct quote. (26) The telling. (27) Harks back to the feeling of nausea mentioned earlier –

checkpoint." I thought to myself, what if he doesn't stop? (28) My heart beat even faster now – if that was at all possible. Should I do something? (29) Should I say something to the soldiers? What could I say? The driver and the passenger hadn't done anything wrong; their only transgression was talking in their native language, Arabic. (30) I stood up in the moving taxi. (31) "Stop!" I shouted inwardly and held my breath until the vehicle slowed down to a stop. I got out. I bent over the guardrail (32) pretending to throw up. The driver waited with the door open. I straightened up and said to him, (33) "Go." He said, "It's a shame, we are almost there." I said to him, "Go. I am sorry. Go." He drove off, (34) and I felt so ashamed.

alludes to resorting to nausea as a pretext for achieving a specific purpose. (28) Intensifying the tension. (29) Introducing a new perspective – if hitherto the reader believed that the situation warranted a drastic step, this sentence presents it from an opposite angle. (30) Projects despair – provides a rationale for forcing the driver to stop. (31) Oxymoron. (32) Links to the nausea motif that emerged at the beginning of the story. Elucidates that nausea is only metaphorical or that it is a result of fear rather than the physical need to vomit. For all that, in the circumstances, it provides a justification for the protagonist's behavior. (33) Reiteration. (34) The coda – return to reality. A universal message about human nature.

Discussion and Elaboration

I explained earlier how emotional stories have the power to bypass an audience's resistance and elicit their engagement. Such is precisely the case here. On one hand, the story pictures an acute situation, presenting it in a "natural" way as dangerous on account of the current social climate; on the other hand, it creates a twist through giving expression to the "thoughts" that race in the protagonist's mind, putting this spontaneous, "natural" interpretation under suspicion.

Thus, at one of its climactic moments (at the check post), the story manages to adulterate the objections that the audience must have formed at that point, provided that, from the outset, the story had been relayed so as to compromise that interpretation. In other words, by eliciting empathy towards the protagonist, who represents the responses prevalent in the current social environment, the narrator could have propelled the audience to independently cast doubt on this "natural" interpretation, or at the very least to question the stigma and prejudice that they, in all likelihood, share with the protagonist.

Through the analysis of the text presented above, one may observe how the elements elaborated in the previous section are fleshed out with the unfolding of the plot. The numbered comments elucidate the purpose of many of the emotive, cognitive, and exemplifying tools employed in the story. Since the scope of this discussion does not allow us to expand on each of these tools, I will present only those elements that are central in promoting the story's agenda.

Rational anchors are the information that locates the story within the situational context, for example, temporal coordinates ("last night") or specifying the route ("from Modi'in to Jersualem"); verbal illustration serves to create a mental picture, as in Comment (9), for example: a visual picture of the taxi's interior including the placement of each of the "players"; the numerous figures of speech are designed to "extort" emotional responses, for example, the oxymoron in Comment (31): "I shouted inwardly."

Regarding Comment (31), one of the female readers of my post said to me in a personal meeting, "Well done! How brave of you to stand up and shout. In your shoes, I would have been completely paralyzed with fear." At first I thought to set her straight, but then decided not to bother: After all, this is how she had experienced the text. In fact, as the writer, I forfeit the ownership of a text the minute it is published. In this respect, I share the approach Barthes (2005) advocates in his article "The Death of the Author," legitimizing the readers' interpretation of texts according to their conceptions and beliefs, even if their reading deviates from the author's design. One could argue that here I shoot myself in the foot by undermining the "method" advanced in this book, but I don't think so. In the final count, what matters is the story's effect on the addressee – not one or the other of its parts being interpreted as the author intended.

The effect produced by my post can also be gauged based on the fact that responses came not only from Facebook users, but through numerous telephone calls, as well as WhatsApp and SMS messages. Even two weeks or more after the post was published, many people whom I met still mentioned it. To me, this is evidence that the story had a strong impact and evoked engagement, thus blurring the boundaries between virtual and actual reality.

Pay attention to the numerous other rhetorical elements in the story, including reiteration, which may take various forms. One is intentional, goal-oriented reiteration, as in Comment (11): "The time was eight p.m. It was dark. The highway was 443." All these and other details had already appeared in the text in one form or another. The repetition is designed to increase tension and create a desired ambience. The other kind of reiteration is contextual, in the socio-cultural sense, and in the story it is so strong that, clearly, one wouldn't be able to decode it if one were not thoroughly familiar with Israeli reality. A person without such knowledge would simply not understand what all the fuss is about.

Another example for such a goal-oriented reiteration is in Comment (6): The driver was listening to Galgalatz – a radio station operated by the Israel Defense Forces. The intention here is to justify the protagonist's trust of the driver and, at the initial stage, and to mitigate the readers' concern about his identity. This information alludes to a number of stigmas and beliefs – one of them is that Arabs do not listen to Galgalatz. If the driver had been listening to Arabic songs, for example, a reader would have said right away: "Are you normal?! Why did you get in that taxi at all if you were all by yourself? And at such a time as this?! Didn't you see the writing on the wall?!"

These questions are also rooted in stigma, because after all, who said that if one listens to Arabic songs one must necessarily be an Arab? And a terrorist to boot? Moreover, was the information that "the driver was listening to Galgalatz" necessary at all? The answer is yes. In terms of the narrative, this information is designed to quell the readers' anxiety. And the purpose of lowering the anxiety level through such an artificial stratagem is to accentuate the surprise later on, when the driver turns out to be an Arab. In a sense, this constitutes a binary opposition, or dichotomy: "Hey, the driver is listening to the IDF radio station, so there's no reason to think he might be dangerous"; but when he speaks in Arabic and then answers a phone call also in Arabic, and then mentions the word "Palestine" several times, the tables are turned: "That driver is dangerous!"

At this point, you must be wondering whether I made up the fact that the driver was listening to the IDF station in order to produce an effect upon the reader. Well, I haven't made anything up. The driver was indeed listening to that station. However, the inclusion of this detail in the story is the result of a goal-oriented choice on my part. Do you remember the section discussing the choice of what to incorporate in a story and what to omit? Potentially, every story can contain innumerable details and information, and we must select what to include and what to leave out. And this is precisely what I did in this case.

This may be a good place to emphasize, in case anyone

has still any doubt left, that this story is true. All the data and facts it recounts are true. Does this mean that this story has taken place in reality? Well, the answer to this question you already know.

This brings me to the next point. What agenda am I trying to promote by means of this story? In truth, the main purpose of this post is not to come up with an eye-opening statement about our society or the complex relationships between individuals against the backdrop of the ongoing conflict, to describe the hardships that we experience on a daily basis, or to undermine the stigmas attached to being an Arab in our society. I am sorry if this comes as a disappointment, but the purpose of this post was unrelated to the narrative itself. I was just trying to prove that I know how to tell a story.

And why did I have to do that? Because at that time, I was running a mass fundraising campaign for the Hebrew edition of this book. And I thought that if I planned to write a book and professed to have the necessary wherewithal, I needed to produce some proof that I knew how to express myself.

I publicized this post also as part of an update on my project, prefacing it with the following comment: "I would like to share with you a post that I have published previously. The reason I want you to read it is that the story it recounts demonstrates the power of storytelling to impart meaning to everything that happens in life. The stories we tell, not reality."

However, my agenda in telling this story here and now, using a different platform, is altogether different. My aim is to validate the central claim of this book, namely, that it is not reality that invests meaning in everything that happens to us in life but the way we interpret it. And our interpretations find expression in stories that we choose to tell, either to ourselves or to those around us. One could even say that stories shape reality; and if so, we must use them to shape reality as we want it to be.

I will now point out some additional elements in the story.

Comment (21): "There are two of them, both men. I am alone, a woman." This information sets the stage for another equation. The tension in the plot is mainly centered on a national rift: an Israeli Jew vs. an Arab. The above passage, however, opens a window to gender-related conflict: a man vs. a woman. In other words, even if you believe that the situation doesn't warrant any concern on the part of the protagonist, because after all, the driver and the other passenger are only speaking in their native language; and even if you think something like "she is a racist, that's all there is to it" – at this point, the situation develops an additional dimension, manifested as an apprehension that any woman would feel on finding herself in an enclosed space, alone with two men, with no obvious escape route. But if you harbor prejudice, as the protagonist appears to do, you will probably add, "and not just any two men, mind you, but Arabs."

Comment (25): (Direct speech) "Idiot.": Importantly, this is the only instance where the protagonist's inward dialog is rendered as direct speech. Hitherto, the story was recounted through the narrator's eyes, and this one-word quotation is an exception: the only place where the protagonist's thoughts are expressed directly in the present tense, as it were. Do you remember what I wrote earlier about this tool: direct quote in the present tense?

Comment (32): The nausea motif. Note that the motif of nausea is present throughout the plot. Initially, it is not clear whether or not the protagonist feels sick, and if so, why. At the beginning (see Comment (16)) nausea is mentioned after the driver twice utters the word "Palestine." Yet at that point it is not obvious if the feeling of nausea originated in fear or as a result of motion sickness. Later on, the narrator states, "I said to the driver, 'Stop. I need to throw up.' I wasn't even sure if I was lying or telling the truth." This sentence raises an additional question: Had the protagonist really been feeling sick? Maybe the whole issue of nausea was only a means for getting the driver to stop? Because it goes without saying that he wouldn't have wanted anyone to throw up in his taxi.

But then comes Comment (32): "pretending to throw up." This shows that whether the protagonist had or had not been actually feeling sick is immaterial; what matters is that, for her, nausea is a pretext for getting the driver to stop, but even more so, to justify her own behavior. The threat to throw up serves as a means to avoid hurting the driver's feelings. It stands to reason that, somewhere deep inside, the protagonist knows that she is wrong, that she is in no danger, but as soon as the taxi comes to a check post – a place that offers an escape route – she makes up her mind. She chooses to risk making a mistake and act as a racist rather than being foolhardy and regretting this later. Do you remember the direct quote? If she stays in the vehicle, maybe she is doing the right thing, but she is also being an idiot. Conversely, if she takes action and gets off, she may be doing a wrong thing, driven by stigma and racism, but within the given social context, she is being wise. Yet, in order to quell the pangs of her conscience and allay the insult she may be inflicting on innocent people, she pretends to throw up. She is trying to prove to the driver that the problem is nausea rather than racism.

Comment (34): The coda. Do you remember what Labov said about the coda, and McKee about a universal message? This is what the closure of the story does. The statement "and I felt so ashamed" brings the reader back to here and now. This sentence contains a universal statement about human nature, relevant to anyone who finds himself in a situation in which he doesn't know what's right and what's wrong; and if he does know what's right, the question remains: Would acting upon this knowledge be the right thing to do in the circumstances? This sentence demonstrates to the reader in an unambiguous, clear-cut way that I (the protagonist) knew that my behavior wasn't really warranted, that it was driven by fear, prejudice, and stigmas, and despite that, I made the choice to act as I did. And that choice made me feel ashamed. But there is also a message for all of us human beings, an insight into human nature. This sentence makes us come to terms with, or even in a way endorses, behavior that is inherently human in a situation fraught with complexities.

Finally, I would like you to carefully go over the questions interspersed throughout the post. Do you remember what I told you about that? A question is a powerful rhetorical tool that elicits engagement in the audience, makes them think and come up with an answer independently.

At this point, some of you must be asking, "What's all that about? Is she in her right senses? All that rigmarole about one puny post?" You must remember, however, that I didn't go out of my way one iota. It's not as if I'd been sitting there, racking my brain about how to tell my story.

In the chapter on promoting agendas, and throughout the entire book, I have incorporated a substantial number of stories, my own and other people's – stories that I had tested based on the schemas and the various steps in effective storytelling. Below I offer an additional example, this time using a post written by a professional, not according to any such schema.

My purpose is to show you two things: first, how one can tell a good story that is not based on a clear-cut, well-defined schema; and second, since you are now adept at the game, that you don't have to adhere to any platform, and can produce stories naturally and without excessive effort.

Remember: schemas are designed to provide pre-built frames for the more popular storytelling genres. You can use them if you are at a loss about what and how to tell. Later on, however, when you have gained more experience and confidence, try your hand at storytelling without using a schema, but at the same time make sure to include the elements that are crucial for promoting your agenda.

The title of the post
"Four marketing tools that even a beggar uses, and you don't!
Or: What can you learn from a beggar about effective marketing?"

Factual grid
In this case, I intertwine two stories into a single narrative, hence the grid is two-pronged.
- On a Thursday night, along with other pedestrians, I was waiting for a green light at an intersection.
- A beggar approached us and said: "Even a dime, in honor of the holy Sabbath."
- I, as well as the other people at the pedestrian crossing, responded generously to the beggar's appeal.

The grid of the story within the superordinate story includes four principles of effective marketing and their explanations:

- A foot in the door
- Like
- Timing
- Illustration

Answers to the guiding questions
Purpose: To write a post on effective marketing that will attract viewers to my blog.
Target audience: A wide list of business owners who intend to market their services independently.
Attention and interest: Through the title and the opening part, both of which create suspense, curiosity, and anticipation.
Engagement: Interspersing the post with questions, using

descriptions to create a visual picture of scene featuring the beggar in the beginning of the story, incorporating another story from the narrator's personal experience.

Value for the addressees: Learning elements essential for successful marketing.

Import: Quality marketing requires familiarity with persuasion theory; less obviously, to get a message across that possibly the addressees need the assistance of a marketing professional.

Below is the resulting story, rendered cohesive through the use of narrative glue and fleshed out to make it worthy of being told. I ensured that the story includes all the linguistic tools conducive to promoting agendas and objectives that appear on the checklist provided earlier. (You are encouraged to identify them independently.)

"Four marketing tools that even a beggar uses, and you don't! Or: What can you learn from a beggar about effective marketing?"

Last Thursday night, along with other pedestrians, I was waiting for a green light at an intersection. Suddenly, a beggar dressed in ragged clothes materialized next to me. Jingling some coins in a red cup, he addressed me thus: "Even a dime. In honor of the holy Sabbath." The place was teeming with people who had just finished their afternoon shopping. Now, I don't know what you usually do in such situations, but I am not overly enthusiastic in handing out alms; on that occasion, however, I found myself dithering. Why? Well, simply because that beggar, unaware and with a single sentence, managed to spur people to action. On my way to and from meetings, I happen to encounter many beggars, but this was one of the few cases in which an appeal for alms elicited an overwhelmingly positive response – and yes, from me too.

When I continued on my way, I pondered what that beggar had done to win such unanimous cooperation. What was it that made me, and other people around me, open our wallets or reach into our pockets and give him money? It appears that the beggar, whether consciously or unintentionally, succeeded in pressing some of the "persuasion buttons" – trivially simple strategies that marketing people routinely implement in their work. These tools are elaborated below, for the benefit of those who promote their services independently without using them – highly recommended.

Foot-in-the-door (FITD) technique (Freedman & Fraser, 1966): This is a well-known compliance tactic that aims at getting a person to agree to a large request by having them agree to a modest request first. The assumption is that agreeing to a small request increases the likelihood of agreeing to a second, larger request. I will not burden you with details, but trust me – this tactic has been empirically tested and found extremely effective. It is premised on the rationale that a person will always find it easier to make a gradual, incremental change than a big, abrupt one.

Note, however, that the beggar used a more sophisticated version of that strategy. His request for "a dime" was arrestingly modest, yet he made all those present, without exception, give him a much larger sum – without the slightest effort! This is because if one has already opened one's wallet or reached into one's pocket, one wouldn't feel comfortable giving such a puny amount.

Like (as in 'similar,' not 'enjoy'): It is known that people tend to be more readily convinced by those similar to them or by those with whom they have something in common. This might take you by surprise, but experiments have shown that a salesperson and a customer being namesakes is sufficient to raise sales rates. But how did the shabbily dressed beggar manage to convey that he and the others present were alike? Merely by saying "In honor of the holy Sabbath," he succeeded in investing his message with a powerful charge and making it clear that even though we are different, there is something that links us together – the Sabbath. He, like everyone else, must prepare for the coming Sabbath, do shopping, cook, and so on. We all await the approach of the Sabbath eve, with everything this entails. It goes without saying that the effect of this tactic would be even more powerful on those who are religiously or traditionally observant.

Timing: The importance of time cannot be overstated. No matter what marketing channel you are using, your key to success is timing! Do you remember "my" old, dilapidated bridge? Well, after the Maccabbiah bridge collapse, practically every media outlet got in touch with me in the hope of producing a news item about the decrepit structure. In what way did the beggar capitalize on this aspect? Simply by making his appeal "in honor of the holy Sabbath," the evening before the Sabbath eve, when everyone was busy stocking up for the weekend.

Illustration (an utterance that gets the message across over and above the overt meaning of its constituent parts): In content marketing, students learn to convey messages through phrases that express the idea better than the combined denotations of their constituent elements. For example, instead of saying "our vehicle is equipped with a very large trunk," it is more effective to describe a potential benefit that the owner of such a vehicle would gain by virtue of its large trunk, for example, "At last you will be able to fit in all your and your children's equipment...and when you have great-grandchildren, also theirs." (I am being facetious here, of course.)

In this case, the phrase "Even a dime" expresses the beggar's privation much more strongly than its component words taken separately. The beggar did not profess, as do many of his colleagues, that he had nothing to eat or that he was hungry and wretched; what he actually said is that even the lowest denomination coin would help him. Can't you just see how desperate he is? Also the intensifier "even" carries a lot of force – see, for example, the headings of this post.

Now, what do you think: If I had told that beggar that he had chosen the wrong occupation – would he have believed me?

You would do well, at this point, to reread the post, but this time with a critical eye and analytically, and identify all the different elements that I have used to transform a simple marketing post into an effective story, one that promotes my agenda and goals.

And once you have finished, tell me: What is the point of this book? Is there a good reason for my call to you to "Tell it right"?

17

The Point Is This

We live in a world where information changes significantly on an ongoing basis. Platforms appear and disappear, but stories stay. Contrary to what people think, we don't communicate by means of words or platforms; these are only tools for transmitting our stories. Even in these times, stories are still what brings us together, and media is merely a vehicle for conveying them.

We tell stories to ourselves all the time; the life of each and every one of us is one big tapestry that we have created with our stories. Our lives are propelled by these stories: we breathe them, act according to them, believe in them, and take every opportunity to tell them to others. At every encounter – at work, in business, at conferences, at home, in a coffee house, in a supermarket, in the street, in our kids' extracurricular activities… what we mainly do is tell stories, constantly and repeatedly. The truth is that sixty-five percent of everything we say during a day is stories. It's not without a reason that some researchers call us *homo narrans*, the human being that tells stories.

If so, why do so many people get uncomfortable and uptight when asked to tell a story? Why is the spontaneous response of these people usually along the following lines: "Why me? Why would I want to tell a story? Am I a writer?" What is the connection between storytelling and success in life and business, and how can it help one to promote one's agenda or achieve one's goals? But mainly, why do so many of us find it so excruciatingly difficult to tell even one satisfactory story? Even after they have realized, internalized, and come to terms with the maxim that storytelling is a superb strategic tool?

Storytelling is part of our genome. Think about it: Since prehistory, humans have been telling stories.

If we think deeply about this, we will realize that cave paintings are the equivalent of modern words, and that cave walls are merely another platform. Is it conceivable that a tribal chief sitting around the fire with his people didn't weave tales? In the era of radio, and later television – the media that replaced the fire around which the tribe would get together – didn't people consume stories? And what are we doing today, in our technological age, be it on Facebook, LinkedIn, or other social media platforms, if not tell stories? And what, exactly, is the nature of TED talks? Aren't these lectures based on storytelling? Isn't it by virtue of the presenters' skills as storytellers that this platform has gained unprecedented popularity worldwide? If one looks at it from this angle, one can see that our current Facebook wall is a perfect counterpart of the cave wall on which our ancestors painted their pictures more than 30,000 years ago.

So what has changed over the past millennia?

Mainly, the tools and the platforms.

If so, at which point along the way did we lose our ability to find and tell a story that would captivate our audiences and make them hang on our every word? And why, in our message-saturated era, at a time when anyone capable of telling a good story can produce a tremendous resonance, did we change from being a *homo narrans* to *cum nulla historia hominum* – people who lack stories, people who don't really know what to tell, how to tell, or why to bother telling at all.

In this book, I have endeavored to provide answers to some of these dilemmas, to guide you, to present you with some ideas, and to divulge some secrets of effective storytelling that can serve you in good stead in life, at work, and in business, by helping you promote your goals and agendas.

The principles and guidelines that I have outlined in this book should be implemented as soon as possible. This is a toolbox essential for anyone who wants to be able to get a message across effectively and convincingly, in a way that will move their audience and motivate them to action in their everyday lives. For those of you whose occupation necessitates conveying content and messages effectively to target audiences, an informed and appropriate use of these tools is indispensable if addressees are to perceive your content as plausible and significant, and if you are to elicit their engagement, which is crucial in today's information-saturated environment.

But it's not yet time for us to part.

Just one more story. A short one. I promise.

18

At Your Fingertips

Sometimes something – a word, a sentence, a story, or a situation – can become engraved in your mind for years and years, and you don't even know why. Has it ever happened to you? It could be something, however unimportant, that someone has told, or a character from a film that you have seen but that left you indifferent, or an episode from a book you have read…

To me this has happened quite a lot. I don't know why, but these things have been part of my life for many years now. One such character that I cannot forget is from Albert Camus's book *The Plague*, which I read almost thirty years ago. The character's name is Joseph Grand.

Grand in French means "big." Joseph the Big. Yet in the book, Joseph is a small and insignificant character: He is a low-ranking and not very successful civil servant in a small town. He cuts a rather pathetic figure, being a writer who has never really written anything that amounted to anything. In his notebook, he keeps revising the first sentence of a novel that in all likelihood will never be finished. He keeps rewriting that sentence over and over again. Every time, Grand starts this sentence from the beginning. More times than one can count, he polishes and polishes the opening sentence of the book that he plans to write. All he does is chase words. He aspires to nothing less than perfection. There is a writer who has never written a book. There is a book that has never been written. There are stories that will never be told. So don't be a Joseph. Do not seek perfection. There is no perfection. Every story that will ever be written will leave room for improvement. Every sentence that you will ever edit will open possibilities for further editing. If I had waited to publish this book until I thought it perfect, it would have never been published. It took me time to absorb this idea.

Why is that? Because for months on end, I kept re-reading, correcting, and editing it. Until one day, a good friend called me and said, "Enough! The internet is full of discussions on storytelling, so it's high time you published that book! Otherwise, instead of being a pioneer in the field, you will find yourself at the end of the line!" Only then did I muster the courage to publish my book.

As for you, if you are dithering, unsure where to start, why not start where you feel the most comfortable? Start small. Take one little step at a time. There is no need to plunge into cold water all at once.

It can be a very short story about something that happened at home – involving the kids, friends, or neighbors. A ludicrous situation at work, a bizarre conversation with a client, a movie, something that you witnessed, something that you've been told, something you've read, something that happened to you in childhood. What it is about is really of no consequence – start with something small that has a point, or with something that you can invest with a meaning that you think may interest others.

Just for practice, arbitrarily, set yourself a purpose.

Write down the factual grid of the story and then start working on the various other stages, as elaborated in this book.

When your story is ready, pass it along to several people who are close to you, either having them read it or telling it to them yourself. If you choose the latter option, remember the illustration element. Try to move your audience. Try to see if your story got through and affected them – touched, amused, or saddened them. Check whether the message has been comprehended, absorbed, and interpreted as you meant it to be. Check whether the story was interesting and whether you have managed to captivate your audience. Ask for feedback and criticism, and hone your story further according to the results of this pilot.

The next step is to upload your story to social media. You can open it either to some of your friends or to everyone. You can preface it with a comment to the effect that this is your first attempt at storytelling or add no comment and just wait for responses; you will find that a good story will elicit quite a few. If your story is built properly, according to the rules, it will win your audience's engagement. On certain sites, such as Facebook, many users will probably not read a story that strikes them as too long. Those who do, however, will respond – provided the story is good. And some will even share it.

Once you've got to that point, tested the water, so to speak, you can plunge into the pool and take on a real task.

To conclude, before we all proceed to working on our life stories, I would like to share with you my first story. That was not my first attempt at storytelling, mind you. As I already mentioned earlier, I had my own blog, and some of the stories presented here are taken from it. When I say "my first story," I mean the first story that I found after the framework presented here had taken root in my mind. It can be said to be my trial story, and my trial story I found on Google. Yes. You are reading right.

Here it is:

When I started my business for story-based marketing counseling and guidance, one of the first things I had to do was open an internet site. A small and basic site, by way of a business card – a so-called image site.

My business approach can be succinctly summarized as: "I would suggest that my clients do not do anything I haven't tried"; accordingly, I decided to build the site on my own. I chose a platform that seemed suitable for my purpose and, by following some straightforward and uncomplicated steps, started building my site. In the simplest possible way. After uploading my logo, I wrote a few lines about the nature of my business and the services I offered, and added a personal touch through the choice of colors and layout – whereupon I got to the point where I was supposed to present "receipts," that is, to show what I have already done as proof of my credentials and capabilities.

The problem was, however, that I hadn't kept any documentation of anything that I had done during my years as an employee. For one, I didn't have a single picture of myself together with the dignitaries whose paths I had crossed as part of my work, among them presidents, prime ministers, actors, entertainers, journalists, and anchors. As a person who is naturally drawn to the shadows of the backstage, I had never felt the need to step into the spotlight directed at those celebrities and thereby to immortalize my moments of glory. This is why, when I opened my business and had to step to the front of the stage in order to relay what I had accomplished in my professional life and provide proof thereof, I had nothing to show for it. Nothing in writing, no pictures, no documents. Only my word.

Totally at a loss, I did what any of you would surely have done in my place. I entered the strongest search engine in Israel, Google, and typed in "Osnat Goaz" in Hebrew.

Luckily, Osnat Goaz is not a common name. Actually, it is a rare name. So much so that I am the only person who bears it in Israel, and therefore probably also in the universe. And that's really a stroke of good luck, because if I were called Cohen, Levi, or any other popular Israeli name, I would have landed on many entries unrelated to myself. In the circumstances, however, my task was fairly simple.

As I had expected, a few things came up that could serve my purpose, and not too trivial either. I found articles that had been published in online Israeli financial journals such as Globus and The Marker, as well as on several other sites. I copied the titles and posted the links to the full texts.

After this, I decided to search in English. After all, I had been in contact with many reporters abroad – rather daringly, I must say – and a company that serviced the Israeli Embassy in Namibia had even once given me an excerpt from a newspaper article where I was quoted.

So I typed in "Osnat Goaz," this time in English, and after scrolling some of my citations – mainly from the time when I worked as a spokeswoman – I saw the following link:

What's THAT?!

I pressed on the link and landed on page 369 of a book entitled *Naomi*, then read the following:

Traveling as Osnat Goaz, an Israeli citizen, I was able to travel around in and out of Israel with very little difficulty. This was alias I used quite often when in Israel.

After leaving Nazareth, I spent three weeks traveling through the West Bank and making contact with the Women of Palestine operations in the many different towns and villages. I also was in contact with several key people in the underground insurgency and Hamas. I then went to the Gaza Strip, met with the Women of Palestine and Hamas, passed on intelligence, and spent a week or so there before returning to Greece and my safe house.

[Haines, K.M. (2009). NAOMI. (p. 369). USA]

In the book, an Arab Muslim woman decided to camouflage herself as an Israeli citizen in order to go in and out of Israel undeterred, to pass on intelligence to the Islamic underground insurgency. Of all the names floating out there in cyberspace, she chose Osnat Goaz – pretending to be me, a person who bears the rarest name in the world!

I don't know if you will be surprised to learn that, after reading the above passage, after looking at the cover, after reading the blurb, the information about the author, and the opening page – I found it hard to regain my composure. I was especially annoyed by the first page, which contained a disclaimer to the effect that any resemblance to actual persons, living or dead, or actual events is purely coincidental. The author also professed to have worked for intelligence agencies and in investigations. That night I couldn't fall asleep. I thought of calling the author and asking him directly, in an attempt to check if that Naomi really existed; to try to find out why the author had chosen to call his protagonist that name – my name! Did he know me? Had he met me?

In the end, I didn't do a thing. I still amuse myself once in a while by playing with the idea of calling him, but he would be highly unlikely to cooperate in any way. In all probability, he would deny having anything to do with me. And that's that. That is the story that I found by punching a few keys on my computer keyboard.

What am I trying to tell you here? What is the point of this story?

That stories can be found everywhere. That a story can pop up any time we put our fingertips to the keyboard. That sometimes we don't need to work hard to find a good story. They are lying about, scattered, under our very noses.

So what are you waiting for?

Go ahead, find your story, and tell it right!

19

Postscript

The term "story," as used in this book, designates content that we pour into different vessels, or molds, that are available and accessible to us. These vessels come in a variety of shapes.

They can take the form of pictures, clips, movies, posts, advertisements, lectures, presentations, conversations, conferences, ceremonies, and more. Whichever vessel may be selected – absolutely any – the focus here is on its content. We can say that the story is the message.

In a famous statement, Bill Gates pronounced content to be king.

Yet Gates surely didn't mean just any content. In our times, in our digital era, in an epoch when we are inundated with content, in our message-saturated age – an ability to stand out, have presence, and gain visibility by virtue of content is getting harder to achieve, and I would go so far as to say is almost unattainable, for most of us.

In other words, Bill Gates's king is completely naked; he is submerged under mounds of content, reams of words, and enormous numbers of messages – visual as well as textual, from advertising, conferences, ceremonial events, encounters. Many of these shouldn't ever have been published, because they are no good. To rescue our king from certain death by drowning, we have no other option but...

To tell a story! And not just any story, but a good one. Because if content is king – a story is its heart!

References

Aristotle. (1976). *Poetics.*

Bakhtin, M.M. (1986). *Speech Genres and Other Late Essays.* Trans. Vern W. McGee. Austin, TX: University of Texas Press.

Barthes, R. (1968). *Elements of Semiology.*

Barthes, R. (1972). *Mythologies.*

Barthes, R. (1977). *Image-Mucis-Text.*

Bialik, H.N. (1975). "Revealment and Concealment in Language." In Alter, R. (ed.) Modern Hebrew Literature (pp. 127–135). New York: Behrman House.

Brooks, P. (1992). "Policing Stories."

Bruner, J. (1987). "Life as Narrative," Social Research 54, (pp. 11–32).

Bruner, J. (1991). "The Narrative Construction of Reality," Critical Inquiry 18 (1), (pp. 1–21).

Bruner, J. (2002). Making stories: *Law, Literature, Life.*

Diengott, N. (2010). *Narrative: An Interdisciplinary Perspective.* [Hebrew].

Eco, U. (1992). *Interpretation and Overinterpretation.*

Elkad-Lehma, I. (2006). *Magic in the Web: Intertext, Reading, and the Development of Thinking*. [Hebrew].

Entman, R.M. (1993). "Framing: Toward Clarification of a Fractured Paradigm," Journal of Communication 43 (4), (pp. 51–58).

Ezer, H. (2010). "Critical Discourse Analysis: Reflective Discourse as a Self-Study Tool by the Research Teacher." In Kupferberg, I. (ed.), Text and Discourse Analysis: A RASHOMON of Research Methods (pp. 165–187). Beer Sheva: Ben-Gurion University of the Negev. [Hebrew].

Ferriss, T. (2007). *The 4-Hour Workweek*.

Foucault, M. (1971). *L'Ordre du Discours*.

Foucault, M. (1980). *What Is an Author?*

Hall, S. (1977). "Culture, the Media and the Ideological Effect." In Curran, J., Gurevitch, M., and Woollacott., J. (eds.), Mass Communication and Society. London: Edward Arnol (pp. 315–348).

Hall, S. (1980). "Encoding/decoding." In Hall, S., Hobson, D., Lowe, A., and Willis, P. (eds.), Culture, Media, Language (pp.128–138). London: Hutchinson.

Hall, S. (1982). "The Rediscovery of 'Ideology': Return of the Repressed in Media Studies." In M. Gurevitch et al. (eds.), Culture, Society, and the Media. London: Methuen & Co. (pp. 56–90).

Hughes, M. (2005). *Buzzmarketing: Get People to Talk about Your Stuff.*

Kupferberg, I. (2010). "Text and discourse analysis." In Kupferberg, I. (ed.), *Text and Discourse Analysis: A RASHOMON of Research Methods* (pp. 13–24). Beer Sheva: Ben-Gurion University of the Negev. [Hebrew].

Labov, W. (1972). *Language in the Inner City.*

Philadelphia: Univ. of. Pennsylvania Press.

Landau, R. (1988). *The Rhetoric of Parliamentary Speeches in Israel.* Tel-Aviv: Akad [Hebrew].

Lévi-Strauss, C. (1962). *The Savage Mind.*

McCombs, M.E. & Shaw, D.L. (1972). "The Agenda-Setting Function of Mass Media," Public Opinion Quarterly 36, (pp. 85–176).

McKee, R. (1997). *Story: Substance, Structure, Style and the Principles of Screenwriting.*

McKenzie, C. & Nelson, J. (2003). "What a Speaker's Choice of Frame Reveals: Reference Points, Frame Selection, and Framing Effects," Psychon Bull Rev 10 (3) (pp. 596–602).

Pirsig, R. (1974). *Zen and the Art of Motorcycle Maintenance: An Inquiry into Values.*

Postman, N. (1985). *Amusing Ourselves to Death: Public Discourse in the Age of Show Business.*

Rimmon-Kenan, S. (1984). *Narrative Fiction: Contemporary Poetics.* [Hebrew].

Rodrigue-Schwarzwald, O. & Sokoloff, M. (1992). *A Hebrew Dictionary of Linguistics and Philology.* Even-Yehuda: D. Reches Publishing Ltd. [Hebrew].

Roeh, I. & Feldman, S. (1984). *The Rhetoric of Front-Page Journalism: How Numbers Contribute to the Melodramatic in Popular Press.* Text 4 (4), (pp. 347–368).

Taleb, N.N. (2001). *Fooled by Randomness: The Hidden Role of Chance in Life and in the Markets.*

Taleb, N.N. (2007). *The Black Swan: The Impact of the Highly Improbable.*

Tversky, A. & Kahneman, D. (1981). "The Framing of Decision and the Psychology of Choice," Science 211, (pp.

453–458).

Tversky, A. & Kahneman, D. (1984). "Choices, Values and Frames," American Psychologist 39 (pp. 341–350, 31a).

Williams, R. (1978). *Keywords*. London: Fontana Paperbacks.

Wodak, R. (2002). "What CDA is about." In Wodak, R. & Meyer, M. (eds.), Methods of Critical Discourse Analysis, London: Sage Pub (pp. 1–13).

* * *

Angelou, M. quote: Retrieved from Goalcast: https://www.goalcast.com

Borrelli, C.: Retrieved from: https://www.chicagotribune.com

Freedman, J.L. & Fraser, S.C. (1966). "Compliance without pressure: The foot-in-the-door technique": Retrieved from: http://faculty.babson.edu/krollag/org

Glass, I. quote: Retrieved from https://www.goodreads.com

Haines, K.M. (2009). *NAOMI*. (p. 369): Retrieved from: https://books.google.co.il

McIntyre, M. & McKee, J.: Retrieved from: https://usflearn.instructure.com

About the Author

O. G. Goaz is a storyteller who specializes in helping individuals, organizations, and businesses find their stories. She gives lectures, leads workshops, and conducts training sessions. Goaz has an MA in Communication and Journalism and over 18 years of experience in the field of marketing communications.

Thank you for reading my book. If you enjoyed it or found it useful, I would be grateful if you would consider leaving a short review on Amazon.

Thank you for your support!

Made in the USA
Middletown, DE
10 May 2021